THE CULTURE OF THE KINGDOM

A Call to the Sermon on the Mount Lifestyle

Billy Humphrey

FORERUNNER PUBLISHING

International House of Prayer Missions Base, Kansas City
IHOP.org

forerunner PUBLISHING

The Culture of the Kingdom: A Call to the Sermon on the Mount Lifestyle
By Billy Humphrey

Published by Forerunner Publishing
International House of Prayer
3535 E. Red Bridge Road
Kansas City, MO 64137
forerunnerpublishing@ihop.org
IHOP.org

Copyright © 2009 by Forerunner Publishing
All rights reserved

This book or parts of this book may not be reproduced in any form, stored in a retrieval system, or transmitted by any means—electronic, mechanical, photocopy, recording, or otherwise—without prior written permission of the publisher, except as provided by United States of America copyright law.

ISBN: 978-0-9823262-2-0

All Scripture quotations, unless otherwise marked, are from *The New King James Version*, copyright © 1979, 1980, 1982 by Thomas Nelson Inc., Publishers. Used by permission.

Scriptures marked as NASB are taken from the *New American Standard Bible* © 1960, 1977 by the Lockman Foundation. Used by permission.

Cover art by Seth Parks
Printed in the United States of America

DEDICATION

I want to dedicate this book to the staff and family of the International House of Prayer–Atlanta. Your steady gaze and continued zeal to see that the fire on the altar never goes out challenge and encourage me daily. It is truly my privilege and honor to serve among a community of people who have unashamedly given themselves to the pursuit of the knowledge of God in the context of ceaseless worship and intercession. The relentless desire of this community to reject the spirit of the age and to live a Sermon on the Mount lifestyle brings fresh courage to my heart to give myself in abandonment for the pleasure of the God-man. You are my heroes. Thank you for your unfailing passion to live *the culture of the kingdom*.

TABLE OF CONTENTS

ACKNOWLEDGMENTS

I want to thank my sweet wife, Maribeth, for her unbelievable encouragement, love and support. You have been so gracious with me when the hours were late and the days were long. You always have encouraged me and have run with me to pursue the path God has set before us, even when it was uncomfortable and crazy. You are the greatest wife, friend, and lover that I could ever imagine.

I want to thank Mike Bickle and Dennis Rouse whose influence has impacted me greatly. Each has laid tracks of righteousness in my heart that will continue to guide me for decades to come.

I am indebted to Art Katz for the standard he has set for us who desire to live an authentic version of Christianity in a post-Christian world. His writings have helped shape some of the thoughts found in this work.

I want to thank Jamie Burns for her tireless efforts in transcribing my sermons and working with me to transform my scattered preaching into a workable transcript. Your commitment to this project was invaluable. You carry this message and are becoming a powerful voice to proclaim it.

FOREWORD

In the Sermon on the Mount, Jesus laid out the constitution of God's kingdom. It establishes the value system that Jesus insists on. It is the litmus test to measure our personal spiritual development and ministry impact. Ministry impact is not measured by the size of our crowds or offerings, but to the degree by which those we minister to walk out these values. The values of the kingdom, as taught in the Sermon on the Mount, should be the most emphasized theme in the teaching ministries in the Body of Christ. They are not for the spiritually advanced but are to be understood as Christianity 101.

God is calling His Bride to embrace these values, that she might become a worthy partner for His Son, ready to rule and reign with Him. It is imperative in this hour that we have messengers who call the Bride to embrace and live these values.

This book is one such call. Billy Humphrey aggressively seeks to embrace and live these values in his own life. It is from the place of fasting and prayer, of serving and giving, that he is urging us, in this generation, to resist the temptation to live a "comfortable" version of Christianity and to embrace and live out the values of the Sermon on the Mount.

After working with us at the International House of Prayer of Kansas City, Billy launched the International House of Prayer–Atlanta. I am delighted that the missions base in Atlanta has established 24/7 worship and prayer in the context of a community dedicated to embracing the Sermon on the Mount lifestyle. I encourage you to take the truths established in this book and, with fasting and prayer, devote yourself in the grace of God to living them out in your life.

Mike Bickle
Director, International House of Prayer of Kansas City

INTRODUCTION

In the spring of 2004, the Lord began to deal with me about the essential need for His Bride to live a Sermon on the Mount lifestyle. It was a short time later that I began to study Matthew 5–7 in order to gain understanding of this centerpiece of Christianity. As I began to consider the concepts of the Sermon on the Mount, like meekness and being poor in spirit, I was cut to the heart. I realized I did not understand the foundations of Christianity and, furthermore, I was not living them. I had considered myself a very committed Christian, yet my version of Christianity resembled the typical Western value system more than it did the culture of Christ. I was living with a Western worldview, with some Christian mentalities mixed in. I was not living by the culture of the kingdom of God. Through the grace of God and by the conviction of the Holy Spirit, God began to deliver me from the sway of the world system. This transformation of my values continues to this day.

In the summer of 2006, after several months of continuous, daily study of the Sermon on the Mount, I preached twelve sermons on the culture of the kingdom as it is laid out in Christ's sermon. The book you are holding has been adapted from these messages. While preparing these messages, the Lord began to impress upon me that there was coming a great collision between the differing value systems in the Church. I began to realize there are many who profess to be citizens of the kingdom of God, yet they do not live according to its culture. It became obvious to me that those who embrace and live the values of the kingdom will one day collide with those who do not embrace Jesus' culture and values. Those who do not embrace the culture of the kingdom, but still call themselves Christians, will find themselves in a collision with Jesus, Himself. Jesus is serious about His people resisting the sway of this world system and embracing His culture.

I believe the Lord is getting ready to remove much of the mixture in the Church. He will deliver His Bride from her conformity to the world system and have for Himself a Church without spot or wrinkle (Eph. 5:27). I believe we are in a season in which it is imperative that we return to the Lord. We must turn to Him with all of our hearts, in intimacy. We must turn to Him with all of our minds, embracing His ways. We must turn to Him with all of our lives and actually live out the values of His kingdom. He wants His Bride to no longer ascribe to a value system that causes her to live in compromise, complacency and opposition to His purposes. He is sounding an alarm to His Church, calling her to return to His standard for her. He is removing the gray areas and bringing His Bride to passionate holiness in love.

At its core, this book is a prophetic call to the Church to turn from the ways of the world system. It is a call to wholeheartedly return to the Lord and to embrace and live the values of the kingdom of God. This work is not an attempt to give an exhaustive commentary on the Sermon on the Mount. Rather, it is geared to pierce our hearts with conviction and call us to live a Sermon on the Mount lifestyle. Throughout this book, we will thoroughly investigate Jesus' teachings regarding the culture and the value system of His kingdom.

My desire is that you would be compelled into a rigorous, devotional study of the values of the kingdom, resulting in the transformation of your heart. My prayer is that you would receive revelation and that grace would be imparted into your heart, thus enabling you to truly live a life worthy of the gospel of Christ. If you desire to see the kingdom of God come and the culture of Christ manifest in your life, read on with a prayerful heart, allowing the Holy Spirit to call you into the culture of the kingdom.

CHAPTER 1
The Kingdom Is at Hand

The Forerunner

In those days John the Baptist came preaching in the wilderness of Judea, and saying, "Repent, for the kingdom of heaven is at hand!" For this is he who was spoken of by the prophet Isaiah, saying: "The voice of one crying in the wilderness: 'Prepare the way of the LORD; make His paths straight.'" Now John himself was clothed in camel's hair, with a leather belt around his waist; and his food was locusts and wild honey. Then Jerusalem, all Judea, and all the region around the Jordan went out to him and were baptized by him in the Jordan, confessing their sins. (Mt. 3:1–4)

Imagine a man dressed in camel skin eating bugs and honey. He is the new prophet who has emerged on the scene. Though he was the son of a priest, he did not follow the conventional approach to ministry. Rather than being raised in the priesthood, he chose the way of the wilderness, giving himself to fasting and prayer for eighteen years, until God sent him forth with a new message. This wild man from the wilderness was, of course, John the Baptist. His appearance was as radical as his message:

"Repent, for the kingdom of heaven is at hand." Those words may seem familiar and even trite to us. However, his proclamation would ignite a spiritual revolution that would change the entire world. What did these words actually mean in the minds of the initial hearers?

John was not only proclaiming that people needed a spiritual awakening; he was also declaring the inauguration of the reign of the Messiah on the earth. "God, in the flesh, is coming to rule," was what the initial hearers understood him to say. This stunning proclamation was what differentiated John from the prophets of old. He was insistent upon the fact that the kingdom of God was being initiated upon the earth and that the rulership of the Messiah was beginning.

When John used the term "at hand," it had unique meaning. The phrase "at hand" is a Jewish idiom. In Hebrew, if you wanted to say something was in front of you, you would say it was "at the face." If you wanted to say it was behind you, you would say it was "at the back." For John to say the kingdom "is at hand," he was saying that the kingdom of God was right there with them, at that moment. What a shock! John was proclaiming that God's chosen ruler was now launching His earthly leadership of the kingdom of God. He was declaring there was a King who was coming to set up God's global empire on the earth.

Of course we now know John was prophesying about Jesus, the Messiah. What the people did not understand in that day was that the One who was to rule was not coming as King at that time; He was coming as a servant. Rather than coming as a conquering warrior, the Messiah would be meek and lowly. John prepared them to embrace an unconventional King by not only proclaiming an unconventional message, but by being an unconventional messenger. His appearance and his approach were not what the masses were expecting. This wild man from the wilderness was God's chosen vessel to introduce His Holy Son to the entire human race. John was a signpost to that generation, indicating that the Messiah was not going to be what people expected. Just as John was unusual in his method and message, so the Messiah would be unusual in His manner and manifestation. This would force the people to change their minds in regard to who they thought God's King should be.

Change Your Mind

> From that time Jesus began to preach and to say, "Repent, for the kingdom of heaven is at hand." (Mt. 4:17)

It is amazing to consider that, when Jesus began to preach, He did not start off preaching volumes of new revelation. He simply preached the same message John had started. The global empire Jesus was initiating was going to cause massive upheaval. He was calling the people to repent so they would be able to embrace His kingdom.

The people believed the Messiah would be a strong king who would come and restore dignity to Israel. They wanted a king who would be powerful and mighty and subdue the nations before them. They were looking for a king who would emancipate them from Roman imperialism and apostate, Jewish leadership. Little did they know that God's chosen King was not coming to free them from earthly tributes but to liberate them from spiritual bondage. When Jesus called them to repent, He was calling them to change their minds about what they had believed

He and His kingdom to be. While He was calling them to righteousness, Jesus was also declaring, "The kingdom is right here with you and is going to manifest through Me. It is not going to be the way you thought it would be. It is going to be set up on a different value system than what you had in mind. You must change the way you think, or you will not be able to receive the kingdom. You must repent!"

It is the same with us today. We must repent. In order for us to embrace the kingdom of God, we must change our minds as to what we believe the kingdom of God to be. Jesus is King, and since the days of His earthly ministry, He has been setting up His kingdom in the earth. Today, His kingdom is manifest in men's hearts, yet there is a glorious day ahead when His kingdom will manifest fully in all the earth. In that day, He will rule upon the earth over all the nations as the King of kings.

The Evidence

> And Jesus went about all Galilee, teaching in their synagogues, preaching the gospel of the kingdom, and healing all kinds of sickness and all kinds of disease among the people. Then His fame went throughout all Syria; and they brought to Him all sick people who were afflicted with various diseases and torments, and those who were demon-possessed, epileptics, and paralytics; and He healed them. Great multitudes followed Him—from Galilee, and from Decapolis, Jerusalem, Judea, and beyond the Jordan. (Mt. 4:23–25)

In order to validate Himself as God's chosen leader, Jesus began to publicly manifest the supernatural power of His kingdom. He began to work substantial signs and wonders among the people. Healings and miracles exploded on the scene. The demonized and paralytics were delivered and set free. Massive crowds began following Him because they had never seen such power released. He was producing tangible evidence of the power of the kingdom that He proclaimed; however, He had yet to explain to them the fabric of His kingdom. He demonstrated power like they had never seen in order to get their attention. These unique demonstrations testified to the uniqueness of the nature of His kingdom. Just as the power that He was manifesting was unlike anything they had ever seen, so the fabric of His kingdom would be unlike anything they had ever experienced.

With perfect strategy, when the crowds had grown vast and the people's interest was piqued, Jesus gathered the multitude to a mountain in order to proclaim to them, for the first time, the core values and mission of His kingdom. The message He proclaimed has come to be known as the Sermon on the Mount. It was within the lines of this sermon that Jesus identified the DNA and culture of the kingdom of God.

The Value System of the Kingdom

Let your light so shine before men, that they may see your good works and glorify your Father in heaven. (Mt. 5:16)

In the Sermon on the Mount, Jesus was establishing the value system for all who would be citizens of His kingdom. Some today believe the Sermon on the Mount is a "high bar" of Christianity not attainable in "real life." They believe it simply serves as a standard of conviction for us. Yet the truth is that it is intended to be the norm for Christian living. The principles of the Sermon on the Mount are not simply good ideas or something to try for a season. They are the prescribed lifestyle for all who are subjects of the kingdom of God. Jesus' intent for expressing the values of His kingdom was to set in place the culture that all believers should not only embrace with their minds as truth, but also walk out in their daily lives.

Conclusion

Throughout the Sermon on the Mount, Jesus reinterpreted wrong teachings that the people had heard from the rabbinical teachers of the law. Six times in the sermon, He said, "You have heard it said, but I say unto you." (Mt. 5:21–22, 27–28, 31–32, 33–34, 38–39, 43–44). He clarified parts of God's law by Holy Spirit revelation through the lens of love. By releasing new revelation to the people, Jesus gave a completely new perspective on familiar teachings. In so doing, He identified the errors in their paradigms and unveiled the true culture of His kingdom.

The people marveled at Jesus' revelation. Never before had they heard anyone speak like He did. So much was new to their ears. His teaching was completely different from what the other teachers taught them. Much of what Jesus taught in the Sermon on the Mount flew in the face of what the Pharisees, the very ones who were supposed to carefully observe and teach the law, had taught the people their entire lives. The Pharisees thought they had God's law figured out. They boiled it down to thousands of rules to keep, yet they ignored God's desire for them to have hearts that were fully His. They were extreme about keeping the externals clean; all the while, they were internally bankrupt. As Jesus said to them, "Woe to you, scribes and Pharisees, hypocrites! For you cleanse the outside of the cup and dish, but inside they are full of extortion and self-indulgence" (Mt. 23:25). They were hypocrites, for they did not do the works they required other men and women to do. They were legalists, who lived without love. Jesus made it clear that His kingdom was not about advocating a rule system for others to live by, but it was about having a heart alive and abandoned to God as He evidenced in His own life. Undoubtedly, Jesus knew that He had created many questions in the minds of His hearers. However, it wasn't until the end of His ministry that He answered their questions by explaining the necessity of love.

CHAPTER 2
The Lens of Love

The Necessity of Love

But I say to you, love. (Mt. 5:44)

The main characteristics of the culture of the kingdom of God are explained in Matthew 6. There we find that Jesus calls us to the lifestyle of giving and serving (Mt. 6:1–4), prayer (Mt. 6:4–13), forgiveness (Mt. 6:14–15), fasting (Mt. 6:16–18), simplicity (Mt. 6:19–21) and trust (Mt. 6:25–34), all issuing from a heart of love. It is important to understand that these are characteristics of one who is a subject of the kingdom of God. They are not a "to-do list" of virtues that we check off. We must approach this lifestyle without the motive of receiving a religious badge or the praise of men. Instead, we must pursue this lifestyle from a heart of genuine love for God and the desire to generously and liberally bless others.

When we consider the characteristics of the kingdom, it becomes obvious they cannot be lived without God intervening in our lives. It is against our sin nature to serve joyfully, give liberally, and forgive those who have wronged us. At a glance, the lifestyle of the Sermon on the Mount can seem overwhelming and impossible to attain; yet, when we experience intimacy with the heart of the Father who extravagantly loves us, our motivations begin to change. Let me illustrate. Many times we read the Bible and consider the directives weighty and challenging. The command to be patient (2 Tim. 2:24) seems impossible to obey for most of us who are dramatically in touch with our desire for instantaneous satisfaction. However, every command in the Scripture is an invitation from God to us. He is inviting us to know Him through the very characteristic He is calling us to live. In other words, it is only through knowing and experiencing the Father's amazing patience with us that we are able to be patient with one another. When God instructs us to be patient, He is actually saying, "Do you know how patient I am with you?" When we realize that His love is exceedingly patient and His heart is longsuffering, we are compelled to be patient with each other.

When Jesus identified the characteristics of the kingdom, the people were stunned. They had to wonder how they could ever live as He was calling them to live. Jesus spent the majority of His three-and-a-half-year teaching ministry emphasizing the concepts that He introduced in the Sermon on the Mount. It wasn't until the Last Supper, however, that He finally answered the question, "How does someone actually live the values of the kingdom of God?"

At the Last Supper, Jesus shared with the disciples the revelations that were the most dear to His heart. As many men near death would do, He had saved the most important realities to emphasize until the very end. In this one setting, He emphasized three different times His "new commandment"—"love one another as I have loved you" (Jn. 13:34, 15:12, 17). This commandment is the epicenter of His value system. In order for anyone to actually live the culture of the kingdom, his heart must be motivated by love. Essentially, Jesus was saying, "You may still think that My kingdom is about keeping a religious to-do list, but it's really about love. My commandment is that you know My love for you in such a deep way that it instructs and compels your heart to love one another, richly and lavishly, and to see one another through love." The experience and understanding of God's love for us is the lens through which we should see all of His teachings as well as His admonitions from the Sermon on the Mount.

The Model of Love

As the Father loved Me, I also have loved you; abide in My love. (Jn. 15:9)

When Jesus commanded us to love one another, He didn't leave us without a model. He said, "I want you to love one another as I have loved you." When we understand His model for love, it begs us to ask the question, "Do I truly know the love that Jesus has for me?" The truth is, we cannot make love happen on our own. We love because the love of God has been shed abroad in our hearts by the Holy Spirit (Rom. 5:5). Jesus demonstrated love for us in the sacrifice of His own life. As He said Himself, "Greater love has no one than this, than to lay down one's life for his friends" (Jn. 15:13). Do we truly comprehend the vast emotions that are burning in the heart of Jesus for us?

Jesus declared He loves us in the same way that the eternal Father loves Him. Can you imagine that Jesus, God in the flesh, is in love with you and me to the same extent and with the same volcanic emotions as the eternal Father is with Him? It is only through knowing and experiencing the emotions of Jesus toward us that we are able to love others. Jesus tells us that once we begin to understand and perceive His love for us, we are to abide in His love and never leave it. Once we begin to taste the realities of His love, we are to continue to give ourselves to knowing His love. The experience of His love impacting our hearts is not something we should ever graduate from. We are to abide in the revelation of His desire for us all the days of our lives. His love is the very foundation from which His entire kingdom emanates. The one who desires to live the values of His kingdom must be rooted and grounded in the revelation of God's lavish love for him.

Love Your Enemy

> But I say to you, love your enemies, bless those who curse you, do good to those who hate you, and pray for those who persecute you, that you may be sons of your Father in heaven. (Mt. 5:44-45)

The Pharisees applied a lens of legalism to the teachings of God. They figured out how to keep the letter of the law without having their hearts alive in love. When Jesus introduced love as the core issue of His kingdom, it demanded that the legalists redefine the way they would approach God. No more could they be justified by keeping the rules without having their hearts immersed in the love of God. Jesus said, "You've heard it said, 'Love your neighbor and hate your enemy', but I say to you, love your enemy." Consider the implications of truthfully and willingly loving your enemy.

How exactly do we define an enemy? An enemy is not defined as a person you hate. Since Jesus calls us to love and not hate, the only possible definition of an enemy is one who is hateful toward you. If we describe our enemies as those that *we* dislike, we have already missed the point. In other words, your enemy is the one who hates you, not the one whom you hate. Hating another is contrary to the value system of the kingdom. As subjects of the kingdom, we are called to reject hate and to embrace love, even loving those who hate us. Yet, who actually loves their enemies?

Jesus instructs us to treat our enemies in a very unique way. He says, "Find out who your enemy is and then intentionally and lavishly give him love." Let me illustrate. Consider the person who hates you. He believes that it is his job in life to send you malicious emails, say evil things about you, and treat you despicably. Imagine he sends you an email that ridicules you and ends with the words, "I hate you!" You then reply, "Please let me know if there is any way that I may serve you. I would like to buy you a coffee. Is there something special you would like?" This hypothetical situation sounds absurd! So often we live contrary to Jesus' admonition to love our enemies. We regularly retaliate when we have been wronged, and we mistreat those who mistreat us. Yet, Jesus says, "Love your enemies, bless those who curse you, do good to those who hate you, and pray for those who spitefully use you and persecute you." This admonition seems ludicrous in today's culture, yet loving our enemies is to be the norm for all those who are subjects of the kingdom of God.

Loving your enemy is something that is impossible for you to do in your own strength. It is not something you can do out of a religious desire to justify yourself before God. The only way one can truly love his enemy is if that one is possessed by the love of God. Most people generally love those whom they like to be around and ignore those who don't like them. Ignoring our enemies is not the same as loving our enemies. In order to love our enemy, our hearts must be motivated by the love of God. We must live life through the lens of love, following Christ's example.

Be Perfect

> Therefore you shall be perfect, just as your Father in heaven is perfect. (Mt. 5:48)

Perhaps the most difficult statement Jesus makes in the entire sermon is the one above. When we read this statement, we immediately begin to feel the weight of the impossible bearing down upon us. It is easy to feel demotivated and defeated when considering the implications of trying to be perfect. Who can be perfect? No one is perfect except God, Himself. It seems as if Jesus is setting us up for failure before we even understand the foundations of His kingdom.

However, we must understand the context of His statement in order to correctly interpret what He is truly saying. The thought that Jesus was conveying begins with verse 43 where He says, "You have heard it said . . . But I say to you, love." The call to be perfect is in the context of the call to love. He was not calling believers to live perfect lives, never making mistakes; He was calling them to Sonship in the revelation of the perfect love of the Father. He was not calling them to perfection in actions; He was calling them to perfection in love. The one who is perfect in love does not fear—"There is no fear in love; but perfect love casts out fear, because fear involves torment. But he who fears has not been made perfect in love" (1 Jn. 4:18). When fear is no longer a motivator in our hearts, we can love and give freely. We are then able to love our enemies because we are not afraid of what they may do to us. We can pursue complete surrender and abandonment to God. When love motivates us, nothing can stop us. The great call of the Sermon on the Mount is to be found alive in love, to be free from fear, and to be abandoned to God.

Conclusion

The strength of our witness to the world is equivalent to the level that we embrace the culture of Christ. When we are living the values of the kingdom we will truly love one another *and* love our enemies. If we love one another, we will bear much fruit (Jn. 15:5, 8), and it will be obvious to all that we are His disciples. If we love, bless, and intercede for the ones who hate us, we will begin to operate in the authority of the kingdom and become a true testimony of Christ to all those who do not know Jesus.

What does it look like to love our enemies? It looks like Jesus. It means, just as Jesus laid down His life, we too must lay down our lives, even for those who hate us. Just as Jesus stretched out His back for our healing, so we too must stretch out our backs in order to become the instruments of healing for the hate in the hearts of others. It is loving an enemy while he lashes out at you. When we love those who hate us, it is a witness to them of the power of the Spirit.

Who can love his enemy? Only a person who has come to know the love of God can love the one who hates him. When physical persecution comes and the torturer is raising a whip over your back, if you look at him through the lens of love, you will say, "I love you, I forgive you." This will be a powerful witness to the heart of your persecutor. We may struggle to understand this in the West, but persecuted Christians throughout the earth live this way every day. This kind of love is foundational to the culture of the kingdom.

CHAPTER 3
The Core Values (Part 1)

The Value System of Jesus and His Followers

> And seeing the multitudes, He went up on a mountain, and when He was seated His disciples came to Him. Then He opened His mouth and taught them, saying, "Blessed..." (Mt. 5:1–3)

The first ten verses of Matthew 5 contain what is commonly called "The Beatitudes." In these verses, Jesus was not giving us a list of dos and don'ts. He simply expressed His heart by revealing what was and is important to Him. While many regard these as a list of rules and regulations, I like to think of them as the core values of the kingdom.

The core values of the kingdom actually make up Jesus' personal value system. It is important to understand this because we can see into His very nature by knowing what it is He deems important and what He is like. The core values are a clear expression of His own personality. They are also the attributes He desires to be manifest in us. To say it another way, they are what He is like, and they are what He likes. As we come to know and embrace the values of His kingdom, we actually come to know His heart and embrace Him.

These core values govern what we, today, would call

Christ's leadership style. No one leads like the Man, Christ Jesus. His leadership is absolutely perfect. To understand His leadership, we must understand that 100 percent of the way He leads is based upon His personal value system: spiritual poverty, mourning, meekness, spiritual hunger, mercy, purity in heart, peace, and persecution for righteousness. Once we appreciate that the core values set the foundation for the kingdom, it is vital that we rightly comprehend what these values actually are. For many, they have become religious clichés; yet they are neither clichés, nor trite. They are the prescribed culture for citizens of the kingdom of God. Therefore, they are supposed to make up our personal value system.

As we look into the core values, one truth becomes very evident; Jesus uses the term "blessed" in a way that is almost foreign to us in the West. He calls lifestyles of spiritual poverty, persecution, mourning, and meekness "blessed." Even at a glance, it is obvious His definition of blessed is not what we, in the Western church, consider to be blessed. Therefore, we must redefine what being blessed means.

Today, most would think of a "blessing" as something that is an obvious and immediate, personal benefit, such as more money, a bigger home, or a job promotion. Jesus, however, is not talking about any of these things. His definition of "blessed" is not mostly about receiving something tangible. When He defines "blessed," He points to spiritual qualities that affect the way we live; qualities that produce benefits like inheriting the earth, seeing God, obtaining mercy. Unfortunately, most in the Western church do not esteem these as valid or important. When it comes to a blessing, most of us look for an immediate, tangible benefit. Jesus, on the contrary, describes blessedness as something besides that which brings us temporal comfort.

If we don't understand the core values of the kingdom, it is unlikely we are actually living by those values. Jesus set up the core values as the normal way of life for those who are citizens of His kingdom. If we are not living by His value system, we must answer the question, "What value system are we living by?" We are living in delusion if we believe that we can live by any other value system than Jesus' and somehow still be citizens of His kingdom. You and I know many who are not living according to Christ's value system, and yet they believe themselves to be Christians. I propose that if we are not living by the value system of the kingdom of God, then we are not actually citizens of the kingdom. If we truly desire to live authentic Christian lives, we must take a close look at Jesus' value system, ask God for revelation to pierce our hearts and allow Jesus' values to become our very own. With these thoughts in mind, let's take a closer look at the core values of the kingdom.

Poor in Spirit

> Blessed are the poor in spirit, for theirs is the kingdom of heaven. (Mt. 5:3)

The words "poor in spirit" are used often in religious circles, but do we actually know what they mean? The idea of living a lifestyle that includes being poor in any way is foreign to the ears of most Christians in the West. We generally believe Jesus wants to make us rich—rich in heart, rich in goods, rich in life. Yet, Jesus said the individual who embraces the value of spiritual poverty, being poor in spirit, receives the kingdom. I believe that the opposite is true as well; those who will not embrace spiritual poverty as a lifestyle will not receive the kingdom.

Being poor in spirit is the recognition that without Jesus we are spiritually destitute and poverty-stricken. It literally gives the idea of one who spiritually lives like a beggar, needy in every way. Living poor in spirit means knowing that we cannot conjure up anything good from within ourselves. Any richness we have is only because of Him. And though He ministers grace to us in His goodness, we are still poor and lost without Him. In other words, if we do not have Jesus, we do not have anything. Another way to say, "blessed are the poor in spirit," is to say "blessed are the spiritually bankrupt," or "blessed are those who realize that they are spiritually impoverished," or "blessed are those who live in recognition of their own barrenness and neediness in this life."

You never graduate from being poor in spirit. It is not something you should desire to see remedied. It is a life of acknowledging your utter dependence upon God for everything. While we are in our physical bodies, we will certainly be poor in spirit. The amazing reward that Jesus promises to those who live poor in spirit is the possession of the kingdom of God. In other words, the blessing that they will receive is the kingdom itself. The entrance to the kingdom of God is only open to the one who embraces the reality of living poor in spirit.

Jesus rebuked the Laodicean church because they believed they were rich and not poor. "So then, because you are lukewarm, and neither cold nor hot, I will vomit you out of My mouth. Because you say, 'I am rich, have become wealthy, and have need of nothing'—and do not know that you are wretched, miserable, poor, blind, and naked—I counsel you to buy from Me gold..." (Rev. 3:16–18). Because they believed they could graduate from spiritual poverty, they grew comfortable; and in their false sense of comfort, they grew lukewarm. They lived in delusion, believing they were well supplied; yet in reality, they were in desperate spiritual need. When Jesus inspected their lives, they were exposed as ones who were in danger of judgment and destruction. His firm but kind correction to them was to repent and zealously seek after God. He was calling them back to a lifestyle of spiritual poverty.

Though God may give us many blessings in this life, we will never move past being poor in spirit. Isaiah 66:2 promises us, "But on this one will I look: on him who is poor and of a contrite spirit, and who trembles at My word." The Lord sets His gaze upon those who embrace spiritual poverty as a lifelong value. He is intently focused on the one who is aware of His spiritual need. Living poor in spirit is the path for all those who will be true citizens of the kingdom of God.

Spiritual Mourning

> Blessed are those who mourn, for they shall be comforted. (Mt. 5:4)

As I said previously, each of the core values is to be embraced as the norm for those who desire to be citizens of the kingdom. How foreign it seems to our ears to think of mourning as a normal part of Christian culture! At a glimpse, we might think that Jesus is describing mourning as the experience of pain and sadness because of suffering loss. While this certainly applies to those who are experiencing loss, spiritual mourning is specifically describing those who live continually longing and aching for God.

Jesus explained in Matthew 9:15 that the days would come when His disciples would live lifestyles of fasting and mourning because He would no longer be with them in a physical way. Jesus was describing the ache in the heart of a person who is desperate for Him. The knowledge that we will be with Him for eternity does not ease our current pain, because our desire to be united with Him is more than our hearts can bear. Spiritual mourning is living all the days of our life in the place of desire, refusing to be satisfied until we are with Him where He is.

The one who experiences spiritual mourning says, "Jesus, I want to be with You. I want to come close to You. My heart is aching for You. I am aching for Your presence." There is a longing within the heart that overrides the emotions and sensibilities. Spiritual mourning is carrying an ache on the inside because of one's intense desire for God. Living in spiritual mourning is living with a lovesick heart. Jesus desires His people to say with the maiden of Song of Solomon, "I am lovesick for my beloved" (Song 5:8).

It is right for us to say to Him, "I miss You." We want to see Him whom we have yet to see. Having felt His presence, we long to touch Him. And though we have heard His voice, we yearn for Him to speak to us face to face. He lives inside of us, yet He is at the right hand of the Father. We have met Him, yet we do not know Him (Job 36:26). The reality of spiritual mourning is living in the tension of being locked inside of time, yet all the while aching to touch eternity and longing to interface with the One who is divine.

For those of us who are of the kingdom of God, all of our lives are lived in this tension. We will long for Him, aching for encounter, until the day we see Him. We must be willing to embrace the inevitable pain and struggle of the life lived in mourning. Many will try to ease the ache of their hearts by finding comforts in other things, like recreation and entertainment. Who will embrace a life of spiritual mourning and refuse to be comforted by the inferior pleasures of this life? Who will embrace the pain of longing in order to experience the only One who can comfort and satisfy our yearning souls?

Just as we are called to live in mourning, longing to be with Jesus, so He longs to be with us. He has been away from us since eternity past. In John 17:24, Jesus prayed to His Father with great desire in His heart that we would be with Him where He is. He is longing for us. Jesus has been a man in love since the onset of creation. His delight has always been with the sons of men (Prov. 8:31). He is a Bridegroom with a lovesick heart, living in mourning until the day when He will finally be with us. Song of Solomon 3:11 describes the day when He will be united with us forever. This is the day when His heart will finally be made glad.

A life of longing is not spent in vain. There is a reward for those who spend their lives in spiritual mourning. Jesus promises that every longing, craving, desire, and ache of the mournful heart will be comforted. When your heart is reaching for God and you are mourning because you feel the veil between you and Jesus more than you feel Him, there is hope for you. You will be comforted. Often, I have spent hours in weeping with a tangible ache in my heart for God. The hunger inside has overwhelmed me many times and left me sobbing in a heap, aching for satisfaction. Have you ever desired to be with Him so much that you literally felt pain emanating from your soul? If you have, you have touched the reality of spiritual mourning. He desires those of His kingdom to ache for Him more than anything else—the way He aches for us. He wants a Bride who desires Him with the same intensity that He desires her. The consolation of my heart when I am in those seasons of mourning is knowing He is not going to leave me in pain. He is going to come to me and fulfill my every craving for Him. There is a day coming when our desire will meet His desire and we will be fully satiated. When we see Him, we will never ache again. When we see Him, He will satisfy every longing and craving of our hearts. Oh, for the day when we finally meet the Lover of our souls, face to face!

There is real comfort awaiting the one who will live this life not allowing his soul to be comforted by anything but God. Satisfaction for the soul is one of the great reaches of the human heart, and is only found by living the values of the kingdom. The pain of mourning is part of the pathway toward the heart's satisfaction. This is a core value of His kingdom—living life in a state of longing until we see Him and are satisfied.

Meekness

> Blessed are the meek, for they shall inherit the earth. (Mt. 5:5)

Many use the phrase, "The meek shall inherit the earth," as a cliché or as a figure of speech. However, this phrase is much more than a figure of speech used by the world. It is a statement made by Christ Himself, and it is a core value of His kingdom. It is, therefore, essential for us to discover what it truly means to be meek. What does authentic meekness look like?

Meekness can be defined as faithfully cultivating a servant's heart in order to benefit others above ourselves in regard to honor, privilege, and position. Jesus is always focused on benefiting others. How different this is from the way people manipulate and maneuver today, in order to attain position and promotion for themselves! How often do we compete with others, striving for privilege and platform? Yet, Jesus calls us to take the low place, the low position. One who lives in meekness intentionally lowers himself in order to promote another. In the kingdom, the one who humbles himself will be exalted (Jas. 4:10). Meekness is always the fastest track to promotion in God's kingdom.

The pursuit of our own preference is the enemy of meekness. When we seek that which we desire before considering the desires of others, we place ourselves before others and operate in opposition to meekness. Paul admonishes us, "Let nothing be done through selfish ambition or conceit, but in lowliness of mind let each esteem others better than himself. Let each of you look out not only for his own interests, but also for the interests of others. Let this mind be in you, which was also in Christ Jesus" (Phil. 2:3–5). When we consider others first, we manifest the very mind of Christ and operate in true meekness.

The word "meek" literally describes one who is humbled by means of affliction. The word picture is one of an individual who has a malady of some kind, which perhaps has left him physically disfigured. It is unusual to see someone with a profound physical ailment strutting in self-assured arrogance. Generally, someone who is suffering physically will walk with his head a little lower and speak a little more softly than others. He lives with a revelation of his need; therefore, instead of parading himself, he manifests meekness from the heart. Meekness, then, is recognizing our severe need for God and living humbly in light of our affliction.

Jesus desires for all the citizens of His kingdom to be

connected to Him through meekness. In Matthew 11:29, Jesus says, "Take My yoke upon you and learn from Me, for I am gentle and lowly [meek] in heart." In other words, "I want you to have this same heart characteristic in you that is in Me. Look at Me and learn from Me. My life is an example of what meekness looks like." Jesus is God in the flesh. It would have been the pinnacle of humiliation for Jesus to have come as the Supreme Potentate of the universe, filling the sky with fire and riding to the earth on angels. He could have commanded all men to bow down to Him because He is God. Even if He came as a king it would have been fully humiliating, because He became a man. But He did not stop there. He came as a baby, born in a barn and laid in a trough where animals eat. And even more humiliating than this, though He was God in the flesh, He allowed the very creation He loves to execute Him so that He could purchase them by His own blood. Jesus' admonition to us is to consider His humility and then embrace it in our own lives.

Jesus wants an entire kingdom of people who live lives of meekness. One of the ways that God works meekness into our hearts is by allowing us to experience problems and challenges with others. God is the One who sets up relational collisions. He will allow us to have relational problems that cause us to argue and assert ourselves in arrogance in order to expose the pride in our hearts. I have come to the conclusion that when I am in an argument and anger and arrogance are manifesting through me, God is actually at work in the midst of my emotional mess. My problem is not with the other person. The Lord has orchestrated the perfect circumstance to expose my lack of meekness. Unbeknownst to me, pride has been hidden deep inside my heart, underneath layers of religious whitewash. The rela-

tional problem is to my benefit and is designed to give me
the opportunity to choose meekness and repent of my arrogance. God uses the most effective means to work meekness in our hearts. Every time we have an interpersonal
conflict with someone, we have the opportunity to oppose
pride and prefer the other person above ourselves. In a conflict, whoever repents first wins. Through repentance and
the refusal to embrace pride, we will find the blessedness of
meekness and will operate as true citizens of the kingdom.

Hunger for Righteousness

> Blessed are those who hunger and thirst for righ-
> teousness, for they shall be filled. (Mt. 5:6)

We have many appetites and desires, but who lives life
truly hungering for righteousness? Hungering for righteousness is not about desiring dull religion. It is about
loving what Jesus loves and hating what Jesus hates. It is
not about desiring a "touch" from God, either. Instead, it
is desiring to live in complete congruity with all that He
is and all that is important to His heart. When we hunger
for righteousness, we hunger for Him.

True hunger for righteousness is not satisfied by going
a little deeper theologically or slightly cleaning up one's
character. Hungering for righteousness is desiring to be
possessed with holiness. Holiness is beautiful. It is the fire
of God burning within the human soul. Living in holiness is a result of being alive and abandoned to the love
of God. The manifestation of holiness is beauty upon you
and pleasure within you. This manifestation is also known
as righteousness.

Let me illustrate this concept. Isaiah 61:10 describes
righteousness as a beautiful robe and extravagant jewels.

Anyone who has ever worn a beautiful, expensive piece of jewelry can attest to the fact that, somehow, the piece makes them feel more beautiful. They are not actually any different. It is the jewelry that has "beautified" them. Imagine such a piece of jewelry is a gift to you from your parents or spouse. You'd carry a sense of beauty upon you and within you when you were wearing it. Inside, your heart would be warmed with pleasure because of the extravagant gift and it would cause you to be drawn to the giver. You are beautified on the outside and filled with pleasure on the inside. This is what righteousness does in your life. When you are clean, you sense the beauty of righteousness upon you and the pleasure of righteousness within you.

Hunger and thirst for righteousness, therefore, comes as a result of having revelation of the pleasure of God. Hungering for righteousness is God's prescription for being filled with the pleasures of God. It is righteous living that brings us in contact with God's beauty imparted to our lives. Living righteously is about experiencing the pleasure of living cleanly. Living cleanly is another way to say living holy, apart from sin. There is no one who lives completely holy in this life. However, the heart that reaches for holiness, desiring to live cleanly, is the heart that experiences spiritual pleasure. "Spiritual pleasure" sounds like an ethereal thing, impossible to be experienced. However, we have access to incredible spiritual pleasures in this life through righteous living. Those who long for these pleasures in this life are actually longing for righteousness. When we experience the pleasure of living righteously, it will transform the way we perceive righteousness and holiness. Most would think living a life of holiness to be the epitome of boredom and dullness. But living righteously enables us to encounter spiritual pleasures that are far more exhilarating than any of the pleasures this world can offer. There is no pleasure as deep and sweet as the pleasure of experiencing the beauty of righteousness.

The counterfeit of righteousness is self-righteousness. It is identifying the dos and don'ts of Christianity and becoming self-confident in religious works. The Bible is clear that all of our righteous acts are as filthy rags (Isa. 64:6). There is a dramatic difference between pompous, self-righteous arrogance and experiencing the pleasures of God by abandoning yourself to Him. One may be able to manufacture a list of religious things to do in order to look righteous compared to everyone else. He may even give himself to faithfully keeping everything on his list. He may look like the most spiritual person, yet his heart will be void of the pleasures of God. Such was the case of the rich young ruler who had obeyed every commandment except the instruction Jesus gave Him—"Go, sell what you have and give to the poor, and you will have treasure in heaven; and come, follow Me" (Mt. 19:21). Because he was so tied to his earthly riches, the young man could not bring himself to obey Jesus. He went away sorrowful.

Hungering for righteousness is not about trying to *look* righteous. It is about longing to be filled with the pleasure of God. The one who makes the list of religious dos and don'ts may keep his list perfectly, yet he will be left empty. Self-righteousness never beautifies and never satisfies. It is the opposite of what God desires for the human heart. There is no righteousness within us, and we are unable to manufacture our own. Only when we hunger and thirst for God's righteousness do we experience the splendor of being filled with righteousness, beauty, and pleasure.

Hungering and thirsting for righteousness is a lifelong

journey. It is more than a momentary desire for God. It is waking up every morning of your life with hunger, thirst, longing, and desire. It is desiring, above all else, to be possessed with the very nature and character of God. Oh, that we would be a people who truly hunger and thirst for Jesus, and Jesus alone! For when we hunger and thirst for righteousness, we hunger and thirst for Him. He desires a people who long for Him and crave Him far more than any other thing in this life. Those who hunger and thirst for righteousness *shall* be filled.

CHAPTER 4
The Core Values (Part 2)

Merciful

> Blessed are the merciful, for they shall obtain mercy. (Mt. 5:7)

In our world today, mercy is lacking. We live in a society where it is normal for those who do wrong to get punished. Most in the Church would agree that when someone is found guilty, he should receive the punishment that is due him, according to the wrong he has committed. Yet mercy is an essential value of the kingdom of God. God's very name is Mercy (Ex. 34:6). Mercy surrounds the throne from which He rules (Ps. 89:14; Isa. 16:5). All the ways of the Lord are mercy (Ps. 25:10). He admonishes us to show mercy joyfully (Rom. 12:8). And in His kingdom, mercy triumphs over judgment (Jas. 2:13) with only those who are merciful obtaining ultimate mercy, the salvation of their souls. Jesus, who is the very manifestation of mercy to the human race, requires those of His kingdom to live mercifully with others. This is only possible through living in a continual revelation of the mercy that has been afforded to us through His sacrifice.

We must come to comprehend the power of mercy in order to have a proper value for it. Many would think judgment and retribution are more powerful instruments of instruction than mercy. Yet, the power of mercy to impact the human heart is much more powerful than judgment.

Let me illustrate. In trying to teach our children the value of telling the truth, my wife and I have always swiftly disciplined our children when they have told a lie or demonstrated rebellion. But the Lord taught my four-year-old son and me the power of mercy on one occasion when my son lied to me. I caught him in the lie, and he understood that he deserved to get punished as a result. Our standard punishment for lying has always been to use the "rod of correction," the way that the book of Proverbs instructs. On this particular day, I felt the Lord impressing me to give my son mercy instead of judgment. I had a picture of Jesus taking my sin and judgment upon Himself, and I knew exactly what I was to do. I explained to my son that though he deserved to get the "rod," I was going to give him mercy.

"What's mercy, Daddy?" he asked.

I said, "It's when you know you are wrong and you deserve punishment, but someone else takes the punishment for you." I reminded him of the story of the cross and how Jesus took our sins upon Himself.

His face, which had been strained at the thought of getting "the rod," now softened as he realized that he was going to receive the gift of mercy. He asked, "Daddy, who is going to get the rod instead of me?"

I looked at him and told him, "I am."

His eyes widened as I rolled back my shorts to expose my thigh. I began to strike my own leg with the "rod" to illustrate Jesus' gift of mercy to us in taking our sin. Each blow was literally driving home the point of God's amazing mercy toward me. Those licks with that little wooden spoon were so painful to me, yet they were nothing compared to the crushing that Jesus willingly took upon himself in order to be united with us.

After a few licks, my son grabbed me and yelled, "No Daddy! Have mercy! Have mercy!" The lesson of mercy from that day is indelibly imprinted upon me, as well as on my son.

Mercy is when gentleness, kindness, and forgiveness are extended to one who deserves judgment. Mercy is not required when someone has done everything right. It is easy to be merciful and kind when someone does not need mercy. Yet, we do not even get the opportunity to show mercy until someone is in need of mercy. It is only when we extend kindness and forgiveness to one who deserves judgment that we actually enter into the blessing of this value of the kingdom. Jesus requires those of His kingdom to "do justice and to love mercy" (Mic. 6:8). We must receive a fresh revelation of the mercy the Lord has given us in order for us to continually extend this grace to others. "Blessed are the merciful, for they shall obtain mercy."

Pure in Heart

Blessed are the pure in heart, for they shall see God. (Mt. 5:8)

Many equate the value of being pure in heart to living a life of sexual purity. While purity in heart will translate into purity in the flesh, this value encompasses much more. Purity in heart has to do with the things that motivate our actions. It has more to do with *why* we do the things we do, than it has to do with *what* we actually do. Purity in heart is having an inner life that is motivated by purity.

For instance, a person may appear to be a great servant, always first to lend a helping hand. However, if the motive of his heart is to be seen and recognized by men or to gain a ministerial promotion, then there is impurity in the motives of his heart. Purity in heart is about having pure motives on the inside that translate to living godly on the outside. A pure heart does not pursue the accolades of men. Self-exaltation is not the motivation for its service. A pure heart gives without regard to self. How often do we serve and give with a hidden motive of being recognized by others or being promoted in our careers or ministries? Those of Jesus' kingdom are required to live with pure motives in regard to all they do.

Paul said, "Let love be without hypocrisy" (Rom. 12:9). This is how a pure heart loves. How is it possible that love could be hypocritical? *Love with hypocrisy* serves and blesses, yet all the while it seeks its own good. *Love without hypocrisy* also serves and blesses, but it seeks the good of someone else. Loving for the good of others is loving from a pure heart; it is loving without hypocrisy. Paul said that love from a pure heart was the primary goal of his preaching and discipleship (1 Tim. 1:5). A pure heart is a clean inner life, free from mixed motives. Whenever we give to others without the motive of receiving something for ourselves in return, we love from pure hearts.

While the pure in heart give, serve, and love without desiring promotion, the reward for the pure in heart is the greatest promotion anyone could ever receive. God promises them dramatic supernatural encounter. Those who are pure in heart will have the reward of seeing God. This speaks specifically of the day that we will see Him and be like Him (1 Jn. 3:2). But even in this age, those who are pure in heart will receive revelation and an increased capacity to experience God. Tasting, experiencing, and seeing God are the rewards given to those who will live pure in heart in this age. God gives us the greatest reward He can offer—Himself. Imagine, all that one must do to "qualify" for massive spiritual encounter is to live with genuine heart motives, authentically desiring the good of others. The reward far outweighs the requirement. The one who will give himself to purity in heart will *see God!* The psalmist said it a little differently in Psalm 24:3–4: "Who may ascend into the hill of the LORD? Or who may stand in His holy place? He who has clean hands and a pure heart."

Peacemakers

> Blessed are the peacemakers, for they shall be called sons of God. (Mt. 5:9)

Jesus was the ultimate peacemaker. He wasn't One who "kept the peace;" He was One who made peace. There is quite a difference between being a peacekeeper and being a peacemaker. Those who keep the peace generally try to avoid conflict, while those who make peace will work through conflict unto a long-term peaceful resolution. One who keeps peace avoids disputes and stirring trouble. Passivity is the hallmark of the peacekeeper. One who makes peace, on the other hand, will rush into a fray and take the necessary measures to ensure the greatest peace for the greatest number, even at the sacrifice of himself. Spiritual violence is the hallmark for the peacemaker (Mt. 11:12). Yet, spiritual violence is not as most believe it to be. It has meekness at its root. It may be hard to comprehend, but the most spiritually violent life is the life that lays down its rights in the spirit of meekness. The one who would be a peacemaker will live the spiritual violence of meekness even unto laying down his own life for the peace of many.

Jesus described Himself as One who did not come to bring peace but a sword (Mt. 10:34–36). He was describing the spiritual violence that was necessary for the Son of God to make peace between God and man. Jesus, the Ultimate Peacemaker, brought peace between God and man through His blood. Once and for all, He abolished the requirement of death for the guilty by satisfying the requirement Himself (Col. 1:20–22). While He made peace between men and God through His own sacrifice on the cross, He brought division between men because of the offense of that same cross. Jesus told those who would follow Him that some of their closest relations would become their enemies, because they would be offended at His sacrifice and the requirement of sacrifice to serve Him. To those who accept Him, He has brought ultimate peace. To those who reject Him, He has brought a sword.

One who would be a peacemaker in this life, embracing this value of Jesus' kingdom, will pursue peace for others at the expense of self. Making peace for men is pursuing that which edifies others. It is about putting aside your own preferences in order to bring blessing to someone else. At the core, being a peacemaker is living the cross—dying to your preferences in order to bless someone else. Paul encouraged the church at Rome to pursue making peace— "Therefore let us pursue the things which make for peace and the things by which one may edify another" (Rom. 14:19). He was explaining to them that the life of making peace was connected to that which builds up and blesses others. In this particular case, he was telling the believers in Rome that they should not do the things that they preferred to do if it would be a source of offense for other believers. A peacemaker will choose the path of meekness, even laying down his life in order to build up and bless others.

When given the choice between doing his own will and giving himself for the benefit of another, the one who is a peacemaker will say with Jesus, "Not my will, but Your will be done." It was in the sacrifice of embracing the cross at the expense of His own will that Jesus purchased peace once and for all. It is in giving ourselves away for the good of another that we receive the distinction and the blessing of being called the sons of God.

Persecuted

> Blessed are those who are persecuted for righteousness' sake, for theirs is the kingdom of heaven. (Mt. 5:10)

This last core value of the kingdom comes as the result of living out the previous seven values. When believers truly live the life of spiritual poverty, mourning, meekness, righteousness, mercy, purity in heart and peacemaking, they will experience persecution. Never has there been a community of believers that has given themselves to living the Sermon on the Mount lifestyle that did not experience the blessedness of persecution. While persecution is rarely experienced by the church in the West, there are many examples throughout history, as well as in our day, of believers who have lived the values of the kingdom of God and have suffered for it.

As I consider this value, the examples of so many individuals from the past flood my mind. There are too many to mention here. Yet one man stands out that I want to make you aware of: Dietrich Bonhoeffer. Bonhoeffer stood against Nazism in Germany, believing that the

Sermon on the Mount was not simply an unattainable standard for Christians, but that it was a culture for all to embrace. During the height of Adolf Hitler's demonic regime, Bonhoeffer ran a Bible school based on living the values of the Sermon on the Mount. He was persecuted and arrested as a result. In one of Hitler's last orders, just two weeks before he killed himself, he called for Bonhoeffer's execution. What a testimony! Bonhoeffer was remembered even by his greatest adversary for living the values of the kingdom! His witness was so powerful that it plagued Hitler enough to have him executed. "Blessed are those who are persecuted for righteousness sake!"

We are almost completely devoid of understanding the "blessedness" of persecution in the West. We tend to think that those who experience character assassinations in public must have deserved it. How rare it is for us to see one who is truly righteous going through defamation, imprisonment, or physical abuse! We are not accustomed to seeing one who is undeserving of persecution experience it. The truth is, however, that there is persecution for those who will live righteously in this life. It is not simply a pronounced blessing from the lips of Jesus; it is a biblical promise! Second Timothy 3:12 says, "Yes, and all who desire to live godly in Christ Jesus *will suffer persecution*" (emphasis added).

Jesus declares that all those who are persecuted *for* righteousness *are* blessed. How foreign that concept seems to us in America! Persecution, a blessing to the American? I don't think so. An American Christian suffering imprisonment and physical torture for the sake of the gospel would be accused by many of doing something to incur such a sentence. We would think he was cursed and not blessed. Jesus proclaims the state of the persecuted as blessed. He describes persecution as a blessing and part of the *normal* values and culture for the subjects of His kingdom. I propose that if we were living the righteousness of the kingdom of God, then we would be experiencing the normal persecution that accompanies this righteousness. The fact that persecution is mostly absent from the church in the West is a sign that the righteousness that draws persecution is absent as well.

Conclusion

As I studied these values over a period of time, I realized that if they were written out in modern language without the Scripture references, most in the West wouldn't believe that these values have anything to do with Christianity. Based on what we hear in the Western church, we would think these values were the opposite of Christianity! For instance, if someone identified the main characteristics of the kingdom of God as:

- Being in dire need of God for everything, even after you get saved, able to do nothing for yourself, living like a spiritual beggar (being poor in spirit);

- Making everyone else great at your own expense, serving others constantly, carrying yourself a little lower and speaking a little less than others, as one who has a physical malady (showing meekness);

- Spending your whole life in weeping, lamenting, and aching because you desire God so acutely and you know you will not be satisfied in this life (mourning);

- Waking up every day of your life desiring to live righteously more than anything else, thirsting for it more than water, hungering for it more than food (hungering and thirsting for righteousness);

- Joyfully forgiving those who are guilty and deserving of judgment, continually being kind and loving toward people who are wicked (being merciful);

- Living authentically from the heart with no motives for promotion, but only motives for the blessing of others (living out of a pure in heart);

- Continually laying down your life for the benefit and peace of others, without regard to your own personal preferences (peacemaking); and

- Experiencing attacks and character assassinations because you have done the right thing, not because you have sinned (experiencing persecution for righteousness' sake).

When written in this way, we would not equate these characteristics with the kingdom of God at all. Yet, they are the true core values of the kingdom. They are Jesus' value system and the expected culture for normal Christianity. These values are so divergent from the norm in the Western church that it begs the question, "What value system are we living by?"

I believe that we have preached another gospel and adhered to the values of another kingdom. We have mass-media Christianity with great marketplace appeal. Yet, the questions remain: How can we truly be living the reality of Christianity if all of the values of Christianity are not observable in us? In other words, if those who claim to be in the kingdom do not practice the value system of the kingdom, then what is the reality of the "Christianity" that they propose to practice? Can our version of Christianity

be authentic if all the values of the kingdom are not resi-
dent in our lives? Is it possible that our current expression
of Christianity is simply a copy without the actuality of
the true culture of the kingdom of God?

CHAPTER 5
The Spirit of the Age

The Course of This World

> We know that we are of God, and the whole world
> lies under the sway of the wicked one. (1 Jn. 5:19)

Whether we realize it or not, there are powerful forces
competing to influence all of the human activity in the
world. There is the influence of the kingdom of God upon
the hearts of men, and there is also the sway of the wicked
one. The Scripture declares that the whole world lies under the "sway" of Satan. The "sway" is referring to Satan's
influence upon the world. At all times, the enemy is attempting to sway men's hearts and minds to agree with
and act out his evil desires. When men give themselves
over to Satan's influence, a course or pathway of wickedness becomes established in the earth. This pathway is
identified in Ephesians 2 as "the course of this world."
Let's look at the first three verses of Ephesians 2:

> And you He made alive, who were dead in trespass-
> es and sins, in which you once walked according to
> the course of this world, according to the prince of
> the power of the air, the spirit who now works in
> the sons of disobedience, among whom also we all
> once conducted ourselves in the lusts of our flesh,

fulfilling the desires of the flesh and of the mind, and were by nature children of wrath, just as the others.

Satan's plan and influence is far more subtle than most might think. The sway of the enemy can be seen in things as simple as trends in fashion, media, entertainment, education, politics, and sports. The enemy does not need to get people to bow down and worship him in order to influence and destroy their lives. He simply needs to get them to embrace a course of life that will draw them away from the value system of the kingdom of God. If the enemy can influence people to embrace his value system, also known as the "spirit of this age," then he can control their lives.

Understanding the Sway

> For we do not wrestle against flesh and blood, but against principalities, against powers, against the rulers of the darkness of this age, against spiritual hosts of wickedness in heavenly places. (Eph. 6:12)

We must understand that we are fighting against principalities and powers who exert their influence upon men. These demonic hosts continually attempt to persuade men to resist righteousness and embrace wickedness. They are assigned to geographic regions (Dan. 10:13, 20) and attempt to manipulate all those within their sphere of influence. When people give themselves to the sway of the principalities in a particular region, they literally manifest the will of the wicked one in that place. As people succumb to the spirit of the age, the principalities and powers over their region are strengthened in their authority over the people's lives.

The influence that principalities and powers initially

exert comes as thoughts and concepts in the minds of men. Once people begin to act out these thoughts in their minds, strongholds begin to form (2 Cor. 10:3–5). Strongholds are simply paradigms people embrace that are in opposition to the ways of God. Every stronghold the enemy builds in the minds of men is designed to corrupt the knowledge of God. Once men embrace these thoughts and concepts, they implement them in society. This is how the enemy's "sway" begins to be manifest. It may initially appear as a fad. Once many begin to embrace a new fad, it becomes a societal trend. These trends are the framework for the course of this world system. The masses embrace trends without much discernment. Because their sinful nature enjoys the current trend, they unknowingly come into agreement with the value system of Satan by simply choosing their personal preferences, and in turn, follow the trend. All the while, their personal preferences are geared to bring pleasure to their flesh without bringing glory to the Lord Jesus or releasing the culture of His kingdom. Through the sway of the world system, Satan draws men into his own value system and away from the value system of the kingdom of God.

Let me illustrate how this works. How is it possible in America, within the span of one generation, that we have moved from abortion being an illegal, criminal act to its becoming a normal part of society, protected by federal law? We have an entire generation in America who has no recollection of the day when abortion was considered murder. Somehow the mass murder of infants within the womb has gone from being a horror to being acceptable in our society. According to Planned Parenthood's research affiliate, over 3,500 children are exterminated daily before they are afforded the opportunity to take their first breath. In the Church, we rarely contemplate the devastating effects of this infant holocaust. Just consider it for a moment: The massacre of the innocent is permitted *and* protected by our own laws. How is it possible that such an atrocity has become commonplace in our society?

Abortion started off as an idea in the mind of the enemy. He caused Pharaoh to kill the infants in the days of Moses and Herod to murder the babies in the days of Jesus (Ex. 1:15-22; Mt. 2:16-18). The widespread destruction of infants has always been the plan of Satan. In recent times, he once again put this plan into the minds of a small number of individuals. Within a short period of time, a much larger group began to embrace this wicked concept. It was something that their flesh wanted, in the name of "freedom" and personal preference. The concept gained strength until many people began to embrace it as the norm. There were court cases in which women demanded the right to destroy their own children before they were born. Somehow, seemingly overnight, this demonic concept became legalized, and the murder of infants in the womb is now protected and legislated by our own government! How could this happen? It happened as a result of people simply following the lusts of their flesh. They gave themselves over to the sway of the spirit of the age in order to fulfill their own desires. Satan can release an idea in the earth and because men are given to follow their carnal desires, the idea can become the norm for the masses in a very short period of time. Once men begin to embrace the influence of the enemy, momentum builds for the continuation of his plan, and men are left to join in or be rejected by society.

Have you ever engaged in a casual conversation with a person who embraced a view that you knew was ungodly and yet you felt the pressure to agree with his ungodly opinion? Even though you did not agree with his vantage point, you felt the pressure to conform to his ungodly mentality. The pressure that you sensed is the influence of the spirit of the age attempting to sway you. Romans 12:2 makes it clear that we are not to be conformed to the spirit of the age, but we are to be transformed, or changed, by renewing our minds. In order for us to live according to the culture of the kingdom, we must be delivered in our minds. The renewing of the mind is a deliverance from thoughts that are in agreement with the sinful nature and the spirit of the age. When our thoughts are no longer in agreement with the spirit of the age, our minds are renewed. The issue that we must deal with is our own conformity to the spirit of the age. God wants to deliver us from conformity in our minds, so that we no longer think as the world thinks and, therefore, no longer act as the world acts. The admonition in Romans 12 is not written to unbelievers; it is written to believers. This should testify to us that it is entirely possible to ascribe to Christianity and yet be completely conformed to the mentalities of the world system. If we are conformed to the mentalities of the spirit of the age, then we will also have actions that are in agreement with the spirit of the age. If we are acting under the sway of the spirit of the age, then we will not manifest the authority of the kingdom of God.

The truth is this: If we are influenced by and acting under the authority of the spirit of the age, we are not living according to the value system of the kingdom. We may label ourselves "Christians," but if we are not operating according to the values of the kingdom of God, it is questionable as to whether or not we are truly citizens of His kingdom. We must intentionally resist the sway of the enemy and pursue the culture of the kingdom of God if we are going to combat the course of this world.

Could it be that many of the things we consider normal today are chiefly influenced by the sway of the spirit of the age and we do not even realize it? Consider the desire to be wealthy that pervades American culture. The "American dream" is founded upon the idea of becoming rich so that you can be at ease and live comfortably. Many in the Church pursue riches in order to find peace in this life. They believe, if they can become financially secure, it will produce joy in their hearts. The Western church has embraced the "American dream" and added a little bit of Jesus to it. We think those who are wealthy are blessed and those who are not are not blessed. Are we able to hear that something as seemingly sacred as the "American dream" is actually the spirit of the age? Or is it that our ears are so in tune with the spirit of the age that the culture of the kingdom seems to be foreign to us? Do we not have ears to hear what the Spirit is saying to us in this hour? There are multiple scriptures that clarify the way we are to think about the pursuit of riches. Consider these verses from Paul's first letter to Timothy: "And having food and clothing, with these we shall be content. But those who desire to be rich fall into temptation and a snare, and into many foolish and harmful lusts which drown men in destruction and perdition. For the love of money is a root of all kinds of evil, for which some have strayed from the faith in their greediness, and pierced themselves through with many sorrows" (1 Tim. 6:8–10).

There are many in the Church today who use the pursuit of riches and the desire to increase personal pleasure through attaining "things" as means to motivate people to give offerings. Titus 1:10–11 describes leaders who teach things they should not teach in order to receive riches for themselves. Often, we hear messages from ministers who claim if we will give more in the offerings, God will "bless" us and make us wealthy. While God desires for us to be lavish givers and it is His plan to bring financial prosperity to His people, financial prosperity is in no way supposed to be used to heap treasures upon ourselves. Furthermore, financial prosperity is not a measure of spirituality. In the Sermon on the Mount, Jesus admonishes us regarding greed, "Do not lay up for yourselves treasures on earth, where moth and rust destroy and where thieves break in and steal; but lay up for yourselves treasures in heaven, where neither moth nor rust destroys and where thieves do not break in and steal" (Mt. 6:19–20). It is clear from His Word that Jesus desires the citizens of His kingdom to focus on the rewards of the age to come rather than to load themselves with temporal treasures.

Overcoming the Sway

> Now all who believed were together, and had all things in common, and sold their possessions and goods, and divided them among all, as anyone had need. So continuing daily with one accord in the temple, and breaking bread from house to house, they ate their food with gladness and simplicity of heart, praising God and having favor with all the people. And the Lord added to the church daily those who were being saved. (Acts 2:44–47)

We must understand that our warfare is against the principalities and powers that influence people to embrace the course of the world system. In order to confront these principalities and powers, the principle issue becomes coming out from under their sway and the influence they exert in the earth.

Spiritual warfare includes a broad base of activity, such as worship, intercession, and prophetic decrees. However, for one to be truly effective in spiritual warfare, he must live a life free from the sway of the spirit of the age. Many desire to have authority over the principalities and powers of the air. Yet, how can an individual have authority over demonic forces if he continually lives influenced by them? In other words, how can we dethrone the enemy when we live under his authority and according to his influence in the earth? In order for us to have authority over the principalities and powers, we must be free from the spirit of the age ourselves. As long as we live under the sway of the spirit of the age, we will have no authority over the principalities and powers that impose the sway. The early church gives us a clear picture of what it looks like to live out from under the sway of the spirit of the age.

In the early church, there was a sharing of life among the believers on a daily basis that transcended even their own private property. They freely sold their own goods and gave to one another as "any" had need. They had "all" things in common. This language and these considerations seem so foreign to us because we view them through our Western, "contemporary Christian" lens. Yet, we must ask ourselves whether we are looking through the lens of the cross or the lens of the sway of the course of the world.

In the West, because of the sway of the wicked one, we have bought into a "culture of isolation," wherein we have placed our own desire for personal comfort above all other things in life. From the basis of this mentality, we have then sought riches and "success" in order to heap upon ourselves personal comforts. This manifests in hoarding things, living isolated lives, sharing rarely, giving minimally and hiding the reality of our hearts from one another. We have given ourselves to protecting our privacy and personal preference at all costs; and, in the "pursuit of happiness," we have abandoned living the culture of the kingdom.

Conclusion

Where is the community of believers who will truly depart from the quest for their own "domestic tranquility" in exchange for living according to the culture of the kingdom of God, embracing a lifestyle where giving things away is exalted above having things for themselves? When believers continue to pursue temporal pleasures and personal preference, not only do they resist the call to live the culture of the kingdom, they also find themselves under the sway of the course of the world, which exalts pleasure and personal preference above every other virtue.

Some of the subtlest aspects of our society are fully influenced by the spirit of the age. Our entertainment culture—which enthrones and idolizes movie stars, rock stars, sex symbols, and athletes—is an obvious example of the sway of the spirit of the age. So many of the things we embrace as normal, or vogue, in pop culture are actually the sway in operation in our culture. What is tragic is that the sway of the spirit of the age influences us in the Church as much as it influences the world. Could it be that the Western church does not manifest the power that the first-century church did because today we are possessed with the spirit of the age?

No one will manifest the authority of the kingdom without being submitted to the value system of the kingdom. The question remains: Who will stand against the sway of the spirit of the age, at the risk of ridicule, in order to see the reality of the kingdom of God released in power upon the earth?

In order for us to overcome the sway of the spirit of the age and truly dethrone the principalities and powers that rule over our cities, we must put off living for our own personal preferences and immediate gratification, and embrace liberal giving and laying down our lives for one another. Only when a community of believers will give themselves in abandonment to the value system of the kingdom of God will it be in a position to demonstrate the authority of God to the principalities and powers in the heavenly places (Eph. 3:10). The authority that Jesus won at the cross is available now to all those who will live according to the value system of the kingdom of God. The community of believers that will get out from under the course of this world system will affect the culture of their society.

We must ask God for grace to identify where we have bought into the subtleties of worldly mentalities and embraced them as the norm for the way we live. I propose that all the facets of our culture that are in opposition to the culture of the kingdom are authored by the spirit of the age. They are mentalities from which we must be delivered. Unless we embrace the kingdom of God and resist the spirit of the age, our society will never experience the manifest power of God.

CHAPTER 6
Immediate Gratification Versus Eternal Rewards

Take heed that you do not do your charitable deeds before men, to be seen by them. Otherwise you have no reward from your Father in heaven. Therefore, when you do a charitable deed, do not sound a trumpet before you as the hypocrites do in the synagogues and in the streets, that they may have glory from men. Assuredly, I say to you, they have their reward. But when you do a charitable deed, do not let your left hand know what your right hand is doing, that your charitable deed may be in secret; and your Father who sees in secret will Himself reward you openly. (Mt. 6:1–4).

The influence of Western culture causes people to focus on meeting their own needs above everything else in life. For most people, the prime pursuit of their entire life is to satisfy the natural longings and cravings of their flesh. To say it plainly, we in the West are focused on gratifying all of our carnal desires as quickly as we can. Microwave dinners, fast-food restaurants, high-speed internet, and television-on-demand sum up the way that we live our lives. We want what we want when we want it, and we don't care what it takes to get it because we want it now. I call this mentality the desire for immediate gratification.

In Matthew 6, Jesus calls us to a lifestyle which is completely opposite to the desire for immediate gratification. He tells us that we are to give, serve, pray, fast, and forgive without looking for any kind of immediate reward. We are to live these characteristics of the kingdom for our "Father who sees in secret." We are not to serve in this life in order to gain status or the approval of men. We are to serve willingly and joyfully, all the while looking for more than a temporal reward. God wants us to serve and give in this life, not for men's approval and praise, but for heaven's pleasure.

When we serve in the Church, what exactly is our motivation for service? Do we serve in order to get noticed by men or to bring pleasure to God's heart? Every person wants affirmation. In fact, it was God who created us with this desire. God wove our frame together, placing inside of us the desire to receive affirmation, acceptance, and love. He wanted us to come in contact with these desires and allow them to compel us into intimacy with Him. Ultimately, we are designed to have the desire for affirmation, acceptance, and love fulfilled by God. However, many of us feel these desires and, unfortunately, pursue temporal comforts and man's praise in order to fulfill them. We tend to work for pleasures that perish and rewards that pass away. The things that we pursue seem likely to fulfill our need for affirmation and love. However, when we pursue immediate gratifications, those are the very things that leave us empty and will eventually disqualify us from receiving eternal rewards.

Let me illustrate. Perhaps an individual has a great desire to be accepted. Because he wants to be accepted, he looks for ways to "serve" in his church. He determines to work extremely hard so that the leadership will notice him and, in turn, he will receive approval and status in men's eyes and perhaps an increased platform for ministry. If his work is unto men for the rewards men give, this is all he will ever receive. He may receive popularity and praise from men, but his reward will end there. There will be many on the Day of judgment who will receive no eternal rewards, though they "served" in the Church and did "good works" for many years. Rather than receiving eternal rewards at the judgment seat of Christ, they will have received their reward in full on the earth because they desired the praise of man rather than the praise of their heavenly Father.

The reward system of the kingdom of God is built upon serving and giving from a heart motivated by love for God, rather than giving and serving motivated by a longing for recognition from man. If a person longs to be noticed and affirmed by men, he will work unto men and not unto God. He will do all that he can to be noticed and praised by people. When men notice his works, they will reward him with affirmation and adulation. When they do affirm him, he will be glad that he was noticed. But when they don't notice his good deeds, he will be hurt that he was unnoticed and unrewarded. It is very sad to live his life in this manner. Though he may have worked hard in this life, he will be disqualified from eternal rewards, having received his reward in full in this life because he sought man's praise and not heaven's pleasure.

The Pharisees who were chiefly interested in appearing spiritual before men blew trumpets to announce their arrival to the synagogues in order to herald their "righteous acts." The entirety of their reward was in another man's blowing the trumpet and a few momentary glances from those passing by. The Father has a heavenly reward system for those who will live their lives for Him. Those who do so will be rewarded openly. The open reward is not speaking of something that we receive in this age. It is a reward that is received in the age to come. Those who receive the open reward will be brought before the myriads of angels and the entire spectrum of believers from all the ages. The Father will look them in the eye with joy flowing from His countenance and say, "Well done!" Those who will pray and serve in secret, without regard to the approval of men, will receive a far greater reward than some badge of supposed spirituality given by man. The eternal Father will reward those believers *openly*. Most of us like to drop the hint to others that we have prayed or served. Yet, when we receive our glory from men through proclaiming our own spirituality, we have received our reward in full.

All of the rewards that are mentioned in the core values are rewards that will be realized in the next age, not in this one. Almost all of the motivation that Jesus uses in the Sermon on the Mount points to a reward system that will not become a reality until the next age. For instance, the meek who will inherit the earth will receive this inheritance in the age to come. Jesus was essentially saying that those who are meek in this age would in fact own everything in the next age. Every stream, every mountain range, all the oceans and beaches will belong to the meek in the age to come. In other words, when Jesus rules the nations in the age to come, the meek of the earth from this age will be on His leadership team. The reward for meekness cannot be emphasized enough! Yet who values and pursues meekness in this life? It is stunning to consider that those who embrace servanthood and humility in this age will be those who partner with Jesus, ruling the nations with Him in the ages to come. Consider it—the meek will actually inherit the earth!

Love as the Motivator

> Love has been perfected among us in this: that we may have boldness in the day of judgment; because as He is, so are we in this world. (1 Jn. 4:17)

The only way that we can live our lives fully for our Father in heaven is by experientially knowing the love that He has for us. When we believe that He is a good Father who loves us and has an inheritance for us, we will live our lives for His pleasure rather than the temporal pleasures of this life.

A person who works his whole life focused on what he can get right now has no real belief in an eternal inheritance. The one who lives without the belief of his eternal inheritance has an orphan mentality. When we have an orphan mentality, we will live our whole lives for immediate gratification because we do not truly believe that we are sons of our Father and that we are going to receive an inheritance. One with an orphan mentality puts off the eternal for the temporal and indulges his flesh with every earthly pleasure he can find. Spiritual orphans live for immediate gratification. They hoard all that they can get in this life because they have no belief in their promised inheritance in the next life. For us to live our lives unto God rather than men, we must understand that the eternal Father loves us deeply and has phenomenal eternal rewards waiting for all those who seek Him in this life (Heb. 11:6). The only way we can resist the desire for immediate gratification and the praise of men is by having an eternal vision of the heavenly Father who loves us and will reward us. We will live unto God if we understand that our greatest good and pleasure in this life will only be realized by living our entire lives unto Him and not unto ourselves. We will live lives unto God if the revelation of His love and goodness towards us is alive in our hearts, compelling and constraining us.

When we are completely given over to the love of God, we will refuse immediate gratification and the praise of men and live our lives unto God. When we work in this age for the praise of men, we are not living motivated by love. Many times a fear of not being noticed or rewarded motivates us to service. We may perform "righteous" acts, yet are we doing them for the praise of men, popularity, platform, and promotion? When we come to know the love that God has for us, we will begin to give ourselves to Him with abandonment and live our lives for Him alone. We will no longer be concerned with pursuing promotion in this life, but we will be chiefly concerned with abandoning ourselves to the love of God.

Consider the disciples of Jesus. With the exception of John, all of the disciples were martyred. They lived in this life as pilgrims and aliens. They understood the value system of the kingdom and the rewards system of the age to come. They were abandoned to the love of God and, therefore, did not pursue temporal pleasures and comforts. They did not give in to the desire for immediate gratification. They were so abandoned in love to God that they laid down their own lives. They were given over to love and lived their lives in this age unto God and not man.

Psalm 84:6 states, "Blessed is the man . . . whose heart is set on pilgrimage." Setting your heart on a pilgrimage means having a heart that is given to the lifelong pursuit of encounter with God. It is setting your heart on a collision course with heaven. The pilgrimage is the journey from the place where you are to the place of encounter with God. It is the pathway to touch Him. When you realize you are simply passing through this world, it will help you not get too comfortable on your way. You will not get too attached to earthly things. By setting your heart on a pilgrimage, you will begin to realize you were not made for this realm or this age. You were made for something more; you were made to be fascinated with God's beauty and presence. You were made to be touched by the Eternal. You were made for God. You were made to interface with the Uncreated One. All the attractions of this life begin to fade. The desires for earthly things cannot compare with the fact that you are made for heaven. When we recognize the splendor that is available to us through encountering heaven, we will leave the pursuit of the temporal in favor of the pursuit of the eternal. When we set our hearts on a pilgrimage, we will leave behind the lesser pleasures and pursuits of this life.

Priestliness

> Coming to Him as to a living stone, rejected indeed by men, but chosen by God and precious, you also, as living stones, are being built up a spiritual house, a holy priesthood, to offer up spiritual sacrifices acceptable to God through Jesus Christ. (1 Pet. 2:4–5)

The core issue of living unto God and not unto men is a reality called priestliness. It is the reason Jesus died and shed His blood for you. All the hosts of heaven have access to the presence of God, yet only human beings, bought by the blood of Jesus, have access to His heart and His emotions. The fact that we have access to the heart of God differentiates us from everything else under all creation.

Being a priest unto God means that our first ministry in life is to His heart. God desires all of His people to understand that He has set His desires upon them, that we alone are what brings delight and pleasure to His heart. When we worship, we may sense the benefit we receive from our adoration of Him, but we may not comprehend the deep pleasure and delight God receives from our love. Yet it is not solely the act of singing or praying that is a ministry to His heart. When we live our lives by His value system, this is a sweetness and blessing to Him. In fact, all that we do in life—if we do it unto God—is a ministry to the heart of God. If we serve in the ministry or work diligently at our job, for the pleasure of God rather than the praise of men, it is a ministry to His heart and brings Him great delight. When we live righteously, manifesting the culture of the kingdom because we want to bring pleasure to Him and bless Him, He is blessed and receives pleasure from us! How could it be that the Infinite receives pleasure from the finite? How could it be that the Uncreated One receives pleasure and delight from His own creation?

Psalm 16:3 says that all His delight is in us, His saints. When we realize that we minister to His heart by operating in the culture of His kingdom, it will fully change our motive for all we do in this life. This is how faithfulness ignites in the hearts of the saints. Instead of trying to be faithful because it seems to be the right thing to do, we live faithfully because we desire to release pleasure in the heart of God. When we understand we delight His heart, our motives for serving, giving, fasting, and prayer will be transformed. When we realize He has given us access to influence His emotions, all of the motive of our hearts will be changed. We will no longer live for the praise of men, but continually live to release pleasure in the heart of our eternal Father. Even our weak attempts to please Him have a dramatic impact upon His heart. The truth is that there is an ache and longing in God's heart for love from people. When we attempt to live righteously in this age, we bring incredible pleasure to Him. In fact, all of our faithful acts in this life bring pleasure to Him. He covered us with the blood of His own Son that we might live a life unto Him, bringing delight to His heart.

Even the seemingly "unspiritual" things we do in this life unto Him are a sweet aroma. For example, if a husband serves his wife around the house and considers it as a ministry unto the Lord, it is just as much an act of priestly service to the heart of God as the hour he spends in prayer each morning. If a child obeys his parents with joy, it is just as much an act of priestly service as the time he spends in intimate worship. The grace to refuse immediate gratification has at its centerpiece the revelation that we are a kingdom of priests. Just as much as we are sons of God and the Bride of Christ, we are also a kingdom of priests unto God. As strange as it may seem, God's heart aches for His people to intimately minister to Him. When we set our lives to minister to Him first, we deeply and intimately bless Him. When we understand who we are as priests unto God, we will live our lives rejecting every other motivation other than pleasing Him first.

Grace in the Trophy Case

Having predestined us to adoption as sons by Jesus Christ to Himself, according to the good pleasure of His will, to the praise of the glory of His grace, by which He has made us accepted in the Beloved. (Eph. 1:5–6)

When we live this life unto God, there is one stunning truth that remains: Any good work we have done that is valuable in the kingdom is only because of His grace (Jn. 15:5). There is a day coming for each of us when we will stand before the eternal Father in full revelation of our sonship and our identity as a Bride to His Son. There will be no veils between God and us. In that day, we will participate in the reward system of the age to come. We will flow back and forth in love with God without any hindrances. Perhaps the angels will look through the "trophy case" of our lives to identify our achievements. They will wonder what it was we accomplished to have been afforded the opportunity to experience such amazing intimacy with God. When they peer into the "trophy case" of our lives, they will find that it is completely empty except for one trophy. When they examine the trophy, they will find the phrase "to the praise of the glory of His grace." It will only be by the grace of God that we are able to live a life worthy of the Lamb and receive eternal rewards. It is the grace of God that makes us what we are in the kingdom of God. Every opportunity He affords us to choose righteousness in this life is because of an invitation in grace. It is God's grace that invites us to choose righteousness and enables us to say, "Yes!" It is by His grace alone that we are able to choose humility, servanthood, fasting, and prayer and refuse the desire for immediate gratification.

God offers us invitations in grace to follow His will all day, every day. His invitation may be to the platform for ministry or to the prison for persecution. Saying yes to God's invitations in grace is how we qualify for the rewards of the age to come. Whether He invites us to the prison or to the palace, the reward is the same if we say yes to His direction for our lives. When we live unto God and not unto man, all that we attain in the kingdom is because of His grace. When we say yes to living the Sermon on the Mount, the final trophy over our life will be "to the praise of the glory of His grace."

Conclusion

The pathway to righteousness in this life and rewards in the age to come is mostly about un-glorified meekness. Many desire earthly accolades because they have no true understanding of the value system of the kingdom of God. The culture of the kingdom instructs us to give ourselves in abandonment to God without respect to what we can receive from men in this life. In the kingdom of God the one who embraces humility is the one who is exalted. The one who serves in secret is the one whom God rewards openly.

When we try to gain men's approval in this age, we forfeit eternal rewards. We have done a massive disservice to new believers by pointing them only toward immediate blessings rather than pointing them to the rewards of the age to come. When we continually point them to attaining immediate blessings in this age, they do not have a proper motive for serving God. We must nourish them on the truths of rejecting temporal comforts and immediate gratifications in order to receive eternal rewards (Mt. 6:19–21). If they do not have a perspective of God's eternal reward system, they will not have a proper motive for serving God in this life. Can you imagine living an entire life serving in the Church, not for the pleasure of heaven, but for the praise of men? The one who does will stand before Him on that day, and He will say, "You never lived unto Me; you did your works to be seen by men. You have already received your reward."

Some would say, "I'm not interested in rewards, I just want Jesus." But it is the desire of the Father to reward those who have diligently sought Him. The Father wants to communicate the level of His delight for us by rewarding us. Consider this: One day the Uncreated God, brimming with pleasure, will look into the eyes of His faithful saints and smile. He will unveil a divinely designed crown that has been woven together in the heavens made of substances from another realm. In that day, it will delight Him to gaze into our eyes and place it on our head. It will be a gift from His heart to ours. In that day, our finiteness will be engulfed with His infiniteness. Our mortality will be swallowed up with immortality. He will clothe us in robes of righteousness and crown us with crowns of heavenly royalty.

There will be deep pleasure released in His heart when He rewards His saints. We will be flowing back and forth in splendor and delight with Him as He crowns us with the rewards of the age to come. All the riches and pleasures of this life are nothing to be compared with the rewards the Father longs to give us. If you will live your life unto God, and not unto man, the Father who is in secret will reward you openly. All those who embrace the culture of the kingdom, living their lives for the pleasure of God, will qualify for eternal rewards and experience this amazing exchange of pleasure and delight.

CHAPTER 7
The Life Lived Out (Part 1)

"Therefore whoever hears these sayings of Mine, and does them, I will liken him to a wise man who built his house on the rock: and the rain descended, the floods came, and the winds blew and beat on that house; and it did not fall, for it was founded on the rock. But everyone who hears these sayings of Mine, and does not do them, will be like a foolish man who built his house on the sand: and the rain descended, the floods came, and the winds blew and beat on that house; and it fell. And great was its fall." And so it was, when Jesus had ended these sayings, that the people were astonished at His teaching. (Mt. 7:24–28).

The crowd who heard Jesus preach the Sermon on the Mount that day had never heard anyone speak as Jesus did. It is likely that they were excited by the authority of His words and struck by the depth of His revelation. It is clear, however, that Jesus did not want to simply wow the crowd with a "new word." He was calling them to a transformation in their lifestyle. He explained that hearing His words without applying them is the epitome of foolishness in this life, while hearing and living them out is the essence of wisdom.

It is the same for us today. The Sermon on the Mount cannot simply be a good study we give ourselves to for a season. It must become a lifestyle we endeavor to live, in the grace of God, through the revelation of love. It must move beyond being a momentary hot topic that we give temporary interest to until the next new revelation comes along. It must be the value system we endeavor to live out the rest of our days in this life. It cannot simply be a "good word" or a nice teaching topic. It must change the way we live our lives, transforming our culture as Christians.

These verses are the anchor of the Sermon on the Mount. The concepts of the core values and the characteristics of the kingdom are clearly identified as issues that can and must be lived out in our lives. We live in a society that has heard the words of Jesus, yet how much of what we hear do we actually see portrayed through the lives of believers? It is clear through this final admonition of the Sermon that there are many who will hear the sayings of Jesus; however, only those who live out the value system of the kingdom will be identified as wise. They alone will be able to stand when they are tested. Those with a sure foundation are those who live the values of the kingdom. It is only those with a sure foundation who will stand through adversity. And it is only those who stand amidst adversity that are living an authentic faith, one that is found to be true when it is tested. In other words, Jesus equates wisdom in this life and authenticity in faith to hearing and living the Sermon on the Mount.

Trembling at His Word

Thus says the Lord: "Heaven is My throne, and earth is My footstool. Where is the house that you will build Me? And where is the place of

My rest? For all those things My hand has made, and all those things exist," says the Lord. "But on this one will I look: on him who is poor and of a contrite spirit, and who trembles at My word." (Isa. 66:1–2)

We have touched on what it means to be poor and contrite (meek) in spirit, but the third facet of this prophecy is directed to those who will "tremble" at His word. The next verses of this prophecy identify that the one who trembles at the word of the Lord is the one who hears it and takes it seriously, embracing it and applying it to his life. The stinging rebuke comes to those who have not trembled at the word of the Lord, "So will I choose their delusions, and bring their fears on them; because, when I called, no one answered, when I spoke they did not hear; but they did evil before My eyes, and chose that in which I do not delight" (Isa. 66:4). This is the same concept Jesus is proclaiming in the last verses of the Sermon on the Mount. He is telling them that His teachings must not merely be smooth sayings in their ears, or words that only challenge their intellects. He is clear that unless they live out that which they have heard, they will not be safe in a time of testing or when turmoil comes.

Has the Lord ever called you into a special season of consecration, a time when you were separated unto Him? Perhaps it was a season where you spent extra time in fasting and prayer and you pulled back from media and other distractions. You leaned into the heart of the Lord, and in that season you sensed the nearness of God. The hand of the Lord was upon you. Certain earthly things began to look less fascinating. Carnal pursuits were no longer as desirable, as the Lord began to release revelation to your heart. He became more alluring, and you found your heart more drawn to the things of the Lord. When these seasons end, many times we experience a subtle letdown in our walk with the Lord. We go back to the day-in and day-out of "normal" Christianity. We don't want our passion to wane, yet somehow it does not stay the same as it was during that special season we had with Him. Are the things that the Lord spoke during that season of consecration any less true when the season of consecration was over? Has God changed? No. God does not change His mind. When He comes near and breathes truth into your heart, He then says, "Be wise with these things I have given you. Hear them and apply them to your life."

In hearing the Sermon on the Mount, have we truly heard the word of the Lord? Has it moved in our understanding from a nice study topic to something that has changed how we live? I'm concerned that we are able to quote scriptures, yet we have no actuality of the verses lived out in our lives. I am concerned that we get excited about Bible studies, new teachings, buying new books and always increasing in knowledge, yet it does not seem to translate into a life lived out. The anchor system of the principles of the kingdom of God is receiving revelation until it becomes the value of our own hearts, changing the way we live. God's values must become realities that are actually lived out, or they are not values. Values that are not lived out are mere theories.

Building on the Rock

> Therefore whoever hears these sayings of Mine, and does them, I will liken him to a wise man who built his house on the rock.(Mt. 7:24)

Jesus never desired for His people to become technicians of terminology without any corresponding reality in their lives. Those who hear the Word but do not actually do the things that they have heard are building, yet it is upon a foundation of sand. The only foundation able to withstand wind and storms is the foundation made of stone. When we do not live out what we have heard, we are building our whole lives on sand. When we begin to live out the realities of the kingdom, we are then building on stone. It is the life lived out that is a foundation of stone beneath us when intense storms come. It is the life lived out that translates into wisdom.

Jesus speaks about the storm, the wind, and the flood in the past tense. He says, "The wind blew, the rain descended and the floods came." Jesus is making it definite that winds, storms, and floods are coming to the house. The house represents our individual lives. Every person will have wind, storms, and floods. In other words, they will have tumults, challenges, temptations, and tensions in this life. Jesus says these are definite realities that will take place in all of our lives. The question becomes: When the storms break in upon your life, have you built wisely?

I am not a builder, but every basement I have ever been in has been made of concrete. I have never been in a basement built of sand. Everyone knows stone makes the best foundation. Sand is a terrible substance to build upon. Hearing and doing Jesus' words is building your life in this age upon the best possible material. Jesus' sayings are not, in and of themselves, the rock for your life. It is the hearing of them *and* the doing of them that translates to rock; anything less is sand.

Many will hear Jesus' sayings and celebrate them. They will even read books and attend seminars about them.

However, if they do not live them out, it is *sand*. We have made a practice of hearing and dissecting all that Jesus said, yet it rarely translates into actuality in our lives. Often, we reinterpret His sayings in order to make them more palatable for us to live by in the West. The mentality becomes, "He didn't really mean all that stuff. He didn't mean you actually have to do something to bless your enemies in order to love them. He meant just ignore them and don't get in a fight with them." When we handle His words in this reckless manner, we are building our lives upon a foundation that is as worthless as sand.

A Storm Is Coming

> "For behold, the day is coming, burning like an oven, and all the proud, yes, all who do wickedly will be stubble. And the day which is coming shall burn them up," says the Lord of hosts. (Mal. 4:1)

Jesus is clear; there is a storm coming! Every person has individual storms that they will have to weather in life, yet have we considered the storm of end-time events that is brewing on the horizon? There is an end-time scenario that includes massive revival as well as the most severe judgments this world has ever experienced. This storm is just in front of us, yet we are almost completely blind to it. God is going to release these things to the planet in a very short period of time. It will disrupt every facet of society. For those of us who live in the West and are given to comfort and personal preference, it will be extremely tumultuous. Persecution is going to break out upon the Church worldwide, and the areas of compromise in our lives, in turn, will be forced to go away. God is going to "hedge us in" with trials and challenges in order to remove all the gray areas from our lives (Hos. 2:6).

When storms of this kind come against us, the question will be: What have you built your life upon? Have you built upon sand or upon rock? There will be many who name the name of Christ right now who will find out in that day that their foundation was not rock; it was sand. It does not matter if we claim to know Him or proclaim His name. If we reinterpret His sayings and live life by another value system, in the day of trial, it will be found out that we have built our lives upon sand. The Bible says at the end of the age that the love of many will grow cold (Mt. 24:12–13). This will result in a great falling away from the faith before the return of the Lord (2 Thes. 2:3). Those who have built their lives upon the rock, hearing and doing the words of Jesus, will stand in that day. Those who have built their lives on sand, hearing and not doing the words of Jesus, will be swept away in the greatest apostasy the Church has ever witnessed.

Conclusion

It is foolishness to subscribe to the values of the kingdom with our minds, but not live them out with our lives. We cannot simply hear the sayings of the Sermon on the Mount and move on from them, looking forward to the next new teaching. The Sermon on the Mount must translate into a life lived out, or we will spend our lives in foolishness. Jesus emphasizes the point that "great will be the fall of that house" which is not built upon the rock. Let's look hard into these words and allow the Spirit of the Lord to break the strongholds in our minds and deliver us from the spirit of the age so that we can align ourselves fully with the kingdom of God.

CHAPTER 8
The Life Lived Out (Part 2)

Therefore whoever hears these sayings of Mine, and does them, I will liken him to a wise man who built his house on the rock: and the rain descended, the floods came, and the winds blew and beat on that house; and it did not fall, for it was founded on the rock. (Mt. 7:24–25)

The one who builds his life upon living out the Sermon on the Mount is the one who is wise. More than that, the individual who embraces and lives this lifestyle will prevail against storms, floods, and winds. As I said in the previous chapter, the storms and floods speak of individual trials that we all face in this life, as well as prophesy of the coming storm of revival and judgment that is imminent at the end of the age. Storms and floods can also be interpreted as attacks of the enemy against our lives.

Throughout the Scripture, floods are used to symbolize the attack of the enemy against God's people (Job 27:20; Ps. 69:1–4; Jer. 46:8–9). Those who live the Sermon on the Mount are called wise and will overcome the enemy's attacks against them. In other words, they will live out the wisdom of God unto dismantling and dethroning the principalities and powers that impose the sway of the evil one upon the world. In this chapter, we will investigate how we can be living testimonies of God's wisdom in the earth so as to dismantle principalities and powers.

God's Eternal Purposes

> To me, the very least of all saints, this grace was given, to preach to the Gentiles the unfathomable riches of Christ, and to bring to light what is the administration of the mystery which for ages has been hidden in God who created all things; so that the manifold wisdom of God might now be made known through the church to the rulers and the authorities [principalities and powers, NKJV] in the heavenly places. This was in accordance with the eternal purpose which He carried out in Christ Jesus our Lord. (Eph. 3:8–11, NASB)

God's plan has always been to use the Church to make His wisdom known to the rulers and authorities in the heavenly places. He has always wanted there to be a demonstration of His own wisdom by His people to the demon authorities in the heavenly realms. In other words, He has made His people the vehicle that He uses to demonstrate His own wisdom to the demon forces controlling the world system. Consider the amazing nobility given to humanity! God, who is infinite, has chosen us to partner with Him in order to demonstrate His own wisdom to demon rulers. The demonstration of His wisdom to the principalities and powers in the heavenly places is part of the eternal purpose for which He has predestined us. It was the cross of Christ that set this plan in motion.

There is an "eternal purpose" for which God has destined His Church. It supersedes all of the other goals, plans, and desires that we make for ourselves in this life. In fascinating perfection, God weaves together many activities in order to perform His eternal purposes. While He is accomplishing His eternal purposes through us, He allows us to sense our partnership with Him. He works through us, utilizing even the most miniscule things in meaningful ways. In other words, when we are obedient to the "small things" of the kingdom of God, God is accomplishing things that have eternal significance in the heavenly realms. All the while He is working to perfect us and to conform our hearts to the image of His Son.

For example, by being generous, we are able to free our hearts from greed and bless someone who has an immediate financial need, yet all the while we are a testimony to the principalities and powers over our region that the kingdom of God has come on the earth. In other words, when men, who are by nature greedy, voluntarily choose to be generous, they have resisted the sway of the wicked one and embraced the values of the kingdom of God. This is, in a very small way, an expression of the kingdom of God coming in the earth. He is a fascinating leader! He is the God who knows how to make one righteous action effectual for multiple kingdom purposes.

Many want to completely understand everything God is doing as it relates to their lives and the Church. They want a "practical" explanation of the purposes of God. However, when we look for a "reasonable" or "practical" explanation of God's purposes, we miss their eternal significance. Many times we demand a "humanly focused" motivation for giving ourselves to the will of God. Instead of something eternal compelling us, we look for a "man-centered" and immediate purpose to give us motivation. We must depart from this mentality. We must determine to give ourselves to all that He desires of us. We must understand that all that He is working in us has implications that reach from the smallest areas of our hearts to the most profound eternal purposes, even things our own minds cannot conceive.

God's plan has always been to use broken and weak people to manifest His wisdom to the principalities and powers. One facet of the manifestation of His wisdom is the demonstration of the power and culture of the kingdom of God in the earth. In other words, God wants to use people to demonstrate, to the principalities and powers of the air, the authority that Jesus purchased through His cross. This authority is not solely for another age. It is to be manifested through people in the earth in this age. This is the authority that the principalities and powers lost through their own rebellion by following Lucifer. God has taken this authority and given it to men through Jesus and His work on the cross. Jesus said, "All authority has been given to me in heaven and on earth ... Go, therefore ... in My Name" (Mt. 28:18–19). When we go in His Name, we go in His authority. How then do we go in His Name, with His authority, in order to demonstrate the wisdom and power of God in the earth?

The Cross, the Wisdom of God

> For the message of the cross is foolishness to those who are perishing, but to us who are being saved it is the power of God ... For since, in the wisdom of God, the world through its wisdom did not know God, it pleased God through the foolishness of the message preached to save those who believe ... but we preach Christ crucified, to the Jews a stumbling block and to the Greeks foolishness,

but to those who are called, both Jews and Greeks,
Christ the power of God and the wisdom of God.
(1 Cor. 1:18–24)

The cross of Christ, the crucifixion of the God-man,
is ultimate foolishness to those who are under the sway of
the world. The idea that God would humble Himself to
the point of servitude and embrace the scandal of execution at the hands of men is utter foolishness to the world;
yet, it is the full wisdom of God. God's wisdom is that
He Himself, through humility and servanthood, would
legally regain that which had been stolen through force
and deception. Jesus went to the cross as the sinless sacrifice. He was fully human, yet fully God, so that He could
redeem for all time all who would believe in Him and take
back the authority over death and hell. It is the fascinating
wisdom of God that the Son of God, through the eternal
Spirit, offered Himself as a payment to ransom mankind.
Through His own death, He conquered Satan, death, hell,
and the grave. You can almost hear the Son of God say,
"This is the wisdom of God; you may kill Me, but in My
death, I will conquer you."

It is, therefore, through the cross that a demonstration
of God's infinite wisdom was made by Christ to the principalities and powers of the air. First Corinthians 2:6–8
says that if "the rulers of this age had understood the wisdom of God . . . they would not have crucified the Lord of
glory," for it is through the cross that they were defeated
once and for all. The principalities and powers clearly did
not understand the wisdom of the cross, nor the power
of it, for had they understood the cross would ultimately
bring about their complete and utter defeat they would
not have crucified the Lord. On the cross, Jesus displayed

the ultimate act of sacrifice by giving Himself for the redemption of mankind. What is the wisdom of the cross? It is the Creator allowing Himself to be murdered by His own creation, not for His own benefit, but for the benefit of those who carried out His murder.

How is it then that God desires for us to demonstrate the wisdom of the cross? It is by continually embracing a lifestyle of humility and servanthood for the benefit of others. When we live the wisdom of the cross, we exhibit selflessness at the highest level. It is selflessness, not for the purpose of a religious badge or title of achievement, but for the purpose of blessing and benefiting others. Laying down one's life for another is the greatest or highest manifestation of love (Jn. 15:13). The highest manifestation of God's wisdom is, therefore, also God's highest manifestation of love. This is the wisdom of the cross. When we embrace the values of the kingdom to such an extent that they become the rule of our heart, we will live the wisdom of the cross. The one who does Jesus' sayings is the one who is wise and who prevails against the storms of the enemy. This lifestyle is the demonstration of the manifold wisdom of God to the principalities and powers.

The Living Demonstration of God's Wisdom

> Having disarmed principalities and powers, He made a public spectacle of them, triumphing over them in it. (Col. 2:15)

This demonstration of God's wisdom through the cross disarmed the principalities and powers and reserved them for their ultimate defeat. This final victory is to be wrought through the Church.

Then I heard a loud voice saying in heaven, "Now

salvation, and strength, and the kingdom of our God, and the power of His Christ have come, for the accuser of our brethren, who accused them before our God day and night, has been cast down. And they overcame him by the blood of the Lamb and by the word of their testimony, and they did not love their lives to the death. (Rev. 12:10–11)

Consider the wisdom and power of God! He has reserved the final defeat of Lucifer to be wrought through weak and broken people. We are crowned with the dignity of overcoming Satan through the blood of the Lamb, the proclamation of our testimony, and not loving our lives unto death.

Conclusion

This ultimate victory over the principalities and powers and Satan, himself, is reserved for the Church. It is an astounding promise, yet it is not apprehended through a single, isolated event. The overcoming of the enemy by the Church in the wisdom of God is only achieved through a life lived out. A life that will embrace the wisdom of the cross in a continual demonstration of selfless sacrifice is the life that demonstrates the wisdom of God to the principalities and powers for their final defeat.

The demonstration of this wisdom is a life given in love for the benefit of others. I call this the "given life." It is the given life that is the reality of the kingdom come on the earth. Living the given life daily demonstrates the wisdom of the cross of Christ. When we begin to live the given life, the very value system that governed Jesus' life begins to govern our own. Living the given life is continually giving yourself for the benefit of others, just as Jesus did. Living a Sermon on the Mount lifestyle will always result in living a life given in love for others. By living the given life, we will demonstrate the wisdom of the cross and, in turn, dethrone the principalities and powers that influence the world through the sway of the wicked one. Only a community of believers who live the values of the kingdom will come out from under their sway, dethrone, and ultimately defeat the principalities and powers that influence the course of this world system.

CHAPTER 9
Spiritual Fantasy and False Prophets

End-Time Power

> And it shall come to pass in the last days, says God, that I will pour out of My Spirit on all flesh; your sons and your daughters shall prophesy . . . I will show wonders in heaven above and signs in the earth beneath . . . (Acts 2:17–19)

Many are familiar with this powerful prophetic word that Peter proclaimed on the day of Pentecost. This prophetic promise had a first layer of fulfillment in Peter's day. However, there is a complete and final fulfillment of these prophetic verses that is yet to come. There is a day when the power of God is going to invade the whole earth. He is going to pour out His Spirit upon all flesh. This glorious outpouring will touch everyone on the planet in some measure.

God is going to raise up an entire generation who will move in the power of the Spirit, with signs, wonders, and miracles. Jesus spoke of this when He said that those who believed in Him would do greater works than He Himself did (Jn. 14:12). It will be a generation moving in the spirit of prophecy, proclaiming the word of the Lord with power that convicts men, cutting them to the heart. Consider an entire generation of believers manifesting dramatic power, doing signs and wonders, and proclaiming the word of God with apostolic power!

I believe this will be a "miracles-on-demand" generation. Cancer and AIDS will regularly bow their knees to the great name of Jesus. When Jesus said, "Greater works than these shall you do," He was not exaggerating. He was releasing a prophetic word by the unction of the Spirit of the Lord. The greater works that Jesus promised will be manifest through His Church. We have not seen this day yet, but it is coming.

We have almost no modern models that give us a picture of the dimension of power that is going to be released in that day. Our most powerful ministries today are but a spark compared to the bonfire of supernatural power that will be released upon the Church at the end of the age. We have some ministries that see people healed regularly, but in that day, the Lord will release His power in a measure never before seen in the earth. The promised outpouring is a real day that is to come in our future.

Spiritual Fantasy

> Most assuredly, I say to you, he who believes in Me, the works that I do He will do also; and greater works than these he will do, because I go to My Father. (Jn. 14:12)

While it is exciting to consider the power of God manifest in such a way, I believe we are living in dramatic "spiritual fantasy" as it relates to the power of God moving through His Church. By spiritual fantasy, I mean we have a lofty vision of the effects of supernatural power released to us that is not congruent with reality. We fantasize that God wants to release power upon us in order to increase our personal sphere, public platform, or greatness in this age. However, God's purposes for releasing power upon the Church have very little to do with increasing our own status or personal comfort. He is going to bring in the great harvest of souls, which will far surpass any harvest the earth has ever seen.

Many believe a breakthrough of power, signs, and wonders is the road to "spiritual success" and tranquility. However, just the opposite is true. When power, signs, and wonders are released upon the people of God, our personal peace will get disrupted to the highest measure. Rather than it becoming the pathway to "spiritual success," when power is released upon a person, that individual will become the target of massive spiritual attack. Demons, human enemies, and even close friends will come against the one who is manifesting power. We may fantasize that more power from heaven will make our lives much easier, but in reality tranquility goes away when power is released in a great measure.

When real power comes upon the Church, the lines of people with needs will be endless. The power to heal the sick is more attractive to the masses than millions of dollars. Millions of dollars cannot heal AIDS, but a people with real power from heaven upon them will continually heal AIDS simply by speaking a word. Masses will line up seeking an answer for their maladies in front of the person who can blow cancer and AIDS out of the body. The Church has never seen that measure of anointing, yet it is coming. When this kind of attention comes to the Bride, persecution will come against her in an unfathomable measure. The church in the West has no concept of this level of persecution.

With the release of power, God will allow His Bride

to experience heightened levels of persecution and problems. Problems are God's protection plan for His Church. When problems come, the people of God grope for Him. Problems cause us to continue to look to Him, rather than trusting in our own abilities or personae. Problems ultimately keep God's people from becoming adversarial towards Him. When power is released, most become puffed up in pride and arrogance. Pride is what repels God. God loves His Bride and will not lose her to pride and arrogance at the end of the age. He is going to allow problems and persecution to buffet her so that she will be able to rightly manage the power released to her. It is certain that God will build His kingdom and release power upon His Church at the end of the age. However, we must recognize that, with this outpouring of power, He will allow great challenges and persecutions to come upon His Church in order to cultivate meekness that she might live dependent upon Him.

We must remove the spiritual fantasy from our minds as it relates to power upon us for ministry. The greater our sphere becomes, the more problems we will incur. God allows this to happen to all those who are close to His heart. Paul the apostle had third heaven revelations; yet because of the amount of revelation he received, God allowed him to be buffeted with a thorn in the flesh. Paul's thorn in the flesh did not cause him to quit having revelations; it kept him from being "exalted above measure," causing Him to completely depend upon God for strength (2 Cor. 12:7).

When God releases power upon His people, it is always to make us servants and not stars in the eyes of men. Jesus had the greatest signs and wonders ministry the world has ever seen, and yet He was the greatest servant of all. The Man with the most powerful ministry the planet has ever experienced was the embodiment of meekness and humility. Every demon targeted Him. Every religious person hated Him. The Son of God, the One who had the greatest power ministry ever, was the most humble Man and the most rejected Man who ever lived.

Moses was second to Jesus in the realm of power. The Bible tells us that he was the most humble man upon the earth at that time (Num. 12:3). God desires meekness and humility to be the guiding values of those He releases His power upon at the end of the age. The release of power upon the Church at the end of the age is not so that individuals can build big ministries and increase in human popularity. Power will be released in order to help conform her to the image of His Son. The Bride is destined to become the servant of all and eventually lay down her life, just as Jesus was the servant of all and laid down His life. Power and problems together are part of God's plan to form humility, meekness, and servanthood in the hearts of His people.

When God puts power upon His people, every demon in hell will make us its target. All those operating in a religious spirit will persecute those manifesting God's power. God uses the pressures of persecution to conquer the one thing that we have authority over in this life—our own heart. He ushers us into persecution in order to make us meek servants walking in love. It is only in this crucible of pressure, problems, and persecution that authentic meekness, servanthood, and humility are forged in our lives.

False Prophets

> Beware of false prophets, who come to you in sheep's clothing, but inwardly they are ravenous wolves. You will know them by their fruits. (Mt. 7:15-16)

Many of us want to move in power, but because we don't have a proper understanding of God's purpose for releasing power, our motivations for desiring power can easily get misplaced. In Matthew 7:13–23, Jesus explains that there are many who will say to Him on the Day of judgment that they did many signs and wonders in His name; yet the terrifying response from the Lord will be to tell them, "Depart from Me, for I never knew you." How is it there will be *many* who will have done signs and wonders in the name of Jesus, yet the Lord will tell them that He does not know them? In these verses, Jesus makes it clear that He is talking about a large group of people when He says *many*. He is specifically referring to people who called Him "Lord" while they lived on the earth. These are individuals who actually did mighty works in His name, yet for some reason they are commanded to depart from Him for eternity. How can that be?

Jesus begins this admonition describing the narrow gate and the difficult way, which lead to life. He says there are many who go through the wide gate and down the broad way, which lead to destruction. He then exhorts us to beware of false prophets, to take notice of them and be cautious. We may think it is easy to identify false prophets because we believe that a false prophet is one who does not look anything like a Christian. Yet Jesus describes the false prophet, not as one who is from a false religion, but as a wolf who comes in sheep's clothing. The words, "false prophet," literally mean one who is a fake or an imposter of a true prophet. Outwardly, he looks like a true prophet, manifesting signs and wonders, yet his inner life exposes the truth of who he really is.

Many are so enamored with power ministries that they have no lens to discern false prophets from true prophets.

They believe that the manifestation of power in a person's ministry is the key feature that determines authenticity in Christ. Jesus makes it clear that there are those who will look just like real prophets and associate themselves with the sheep, yet inwardly they are like "ravenous wolves." The word "ravenous" can also be translated as "one who is a swindler or greedy." Therefore, false prophets can be identified as ones who are greedy for money. They want to swindle people by the use of the gospel. The word, "ravenous," can also be translated "rapacious." This gives the picture of an animal that preys and lives off other animals. A false prophet is one who uses the name of Christ and uses his sphere in ministry for his own benefit. He does not look out for the good of the people but only for his own interests. He uses the ministry as a means to financial gain and personal prowess. This is what Paul warned the elders from Ephesus of in Acts 20:29–30. He told them to beware of men who would not look after the good of the flock but would draw them after themselves for their own benefit.

Jesus further tells us that the fruit of the false prophet is what will make it easy to identify Him. He says that a good tree will bear good fruit and a bad tree will bear bad fruit (Mt. 7:16–20). A false prophet is one who bears bad fruit. Could it be that we have wrongly assessed good fruit and bad fruit? Many believe that power manifestations are a sign of good fruit. However, false prophets are able to manifest power in the name of Jesus. We are only able to identify them as false because they bear bad fruit. The false prophet bears the bad fruit of selfish ambition, greed, and the desire for personal gain at the expense of others. He does not bear the fruit of righteousness. The fruit he bears is the exact opposite of the value system of the kingdom and the character of Christ. Christ laid down His life for the blessing of the whole world; the false prophet uses and devours men for the benefit of himself.

When Jesus makes the fearsome statements in verses 21–23, He describes the false prophets that He just warned of in verses 15–20. We must be instructed by Jesus' warning. He describes a conversation that He will have with real people on the Day of judgment. They will stand before Him on that day, and He will tell them to depart from Him. They will depart, not because they did not manifest power, but because they did not live out the values of His kingdom in meekness and servanthood. The stunning truth remains: There is a pathway to miracles and power that does not lead to intimacy with Jesus and, in the end, will bring men to destruction. When we pursue the power of God for the purpose of increasing our own personae, we begin to move down the same path as those who will be categorized as false prophets at the end of the age. When love is not the motivating factor for desiring to do miracles, signs, and wonders, it is an errant pursuit of power, which Jesus identifies as "practicing lawlessness."

Conclusion

How many models do we have in the Western church of ministries that manifest prophetic power and simultaneously embrace the authentic character of Christ? What is it that differentiates a true power and prophetic ministry from one that is false? False prophets are those who have tapped into the power realm and prophesy in the name of Jesus. They do all manner of signs, wonders, and miracles. On the outside, by all accounts, they look like "sheep." Yet because they are divorced from the culture of the kingdom and live motivated by greed, using people for their own gain, Jesus calls them "false."

It is imperative to gain Jesus' perspective as it relates to the manifestation of the power of His kingdom. We tend to exalt an individual's "anointing" without regard to whether or not the character of Christ is formed within him. We will endure and embrace someone who doesn't have the character of Christ, if he has a little bit of the "anointing." If the truth be told, we flock to ministers who manifest power, without any knowledge of their character. Jesus exalts the fruit of righteousness as the core issue without regard to power manifestations. We must change our mentality of what we deem to be good and bad fruit, ridding ourselves of spiritual fantasy and embracing Jesus' value system as it relates to power being released upon us at the end of the age.

Great power is coming upon the Church! It is essential that those who manifest the power of the kingdom embrace the value system of the kingdom so that they may stand in righteousness amidst great apostasy and unprecedented persecution. Oh, that we would be a people who not only manifest the power of the kingdom, but live out the value system of the King!

CHAPTER 10
Living Generously

Your Father who sees in secret will Himself reward you openly. (Mt. 6:4)

In Matthew 6, Jesus identifies seven characteristics of the kingdom of God. While this is not an exhaustive list of kingdom characteristics, it does give us a picture of the lifestyle someone will lead who is living by the values of the kingdom. As I have mentioned before, these characteristics include charitable deeds, which are understood as giving and serving (Mt. 6:1-4); the lifestyle of prayer (Mt. 6:4–13); forgiveness (Mt. 6:14–15); fasting (Mt. 6:16–18); simplicity (Mt. 6:19–21); and trust (Mt. 6:25–34). These characteristics make up the nucleus of what we identify as the "fasted lifestyle."

There is one principle that is to govern our hearts as we live these characteristics. We are to live to bring pleasure to the heart of God rather than to earn the approval of men. As we live aiming to bring pleasure to the heart of God, we will simultaneously attain the greatest good for others. We will be empowered to live by this principle if we will focus on the rewards of the age to come rather than the "pleasures" of this life. This is the lifestyle that qualifies us to receive rewards from our good Father who loves to reward His children openly (Mt. 6:4, 6, 18; Lk. 12:32).

Treasures in Heaven

Do not lay up for yourselves treasures on earth, where moth and rust destroy and where thieves break in and steal; but lay up for yourselves treasures in heaven, where neither moth nor rust destroys and where thieves do not break in and steal. For where your treasure is, there your heart will be also. (Mt. 6:19–21)

In these verses, Jesus gives us a commentary on resisting the desire for immediate gratification in light of the rewards of the age to come. These verses, along with verses 22–24, are one seamless thought, explaining the whole concept of this chapter.

Often, we have heard verses 19 and 20 quoted during offering messages. A minister might make an appeal that we should lay up treasures in heaven by putting more money in the offering. However, this verse is not primarily about giving finances in an offering. Certainly giving an offering could fall under the main idea of this verse, but financial giving is not all that Jesus is talking about here. He is explaining what it looks like to embrace the values of the Sermon on the Mount, specifically living to please God, rather than yourself, by serving and blessing others. It is this lifestyle that "lays up treasures in heaven."

Someone who lays up treasures in heaven serves, gives, prays, fasts, and forgives while rejecting the desires for immediate gratification and the praise of men. They live this way because they are in love with God. The treasure they will receive will not be a momentary reward. The Father who sees in secret will reward them that day before the hosts of heaven and billions of glorified saints. Laying up for yourselves treasures in heaven is not specifically talking about giving money and getting more money back at a later time. Laying up treasures is embracing the Sermon on the Mount lifestyle unto receiving incomprehensible rewards in the age to come.

The Good Eye

> The lamp of the body is the eye. If therefore your eye is good, your whole body will be full of light. But if your eye is bad, your whole body will be full of darkness. If therefore the light that is in you is darkness, how great is that darkness! (Mt. 6:22–23)

Jesus says that if our eye is good, our whole body will be full of light. What does Jesus mean when He discusses the "good eye?" He is saying that, if we will set our eye on "good things," light will flood our entire body. Having a good eye is more than making sure that you do not look at anything lustful or perverse. The good eye is a paradigm, governing the way we think and act in this age. One with a good eye is focused on living for the pleasure of God whereby he will receive rewards and eternal treasures in the age to come. Jesus is talking about a mindset that governs our hearts and our actions in this life.

Living with a good eye is setting your mind upon things above rather than things on the earth (Col. 3:1–2). When we live focused on the eternal rather than the momentary, we will be able to live the values of the kingdom with free hearts. It becomes easy to serve and give to others when we realize there is another age coming in which the saints will rule and reign with Jesus upon the earth (Rev. 5:10). Living with an eternal perspective is living with a good eye.

The "bad eye" is also a mindset. The bad eye is the eye

that is focused upon the temporal. It is the heart that is chiefly concerned with satisfying the desires of the flesh, here and now. One with a bad eye is living motivated by how to get earthly provision and pleasures. If you consider the entire discussion of Matthew 6 in its context, the bad eye focuses on the temporal while the good eye focuses on the eternal. In essence Jesus is saying, "If you want light to flood you, if you want to experience the delight of heaven and the presence of God, you must set your heart on the kingdom that is to come and the rewards of the next age. Only then will you experience My light flooding your entire being. But if you primarily set your heart on attaining carnal pleasures and the praise of men, then your eye is bad, and your whole body will be full of darkness."

It is possible to build large ministries that have a big sphere of influence, yet if we are completely focused on how great they will be in this age, we will be told at the judgment seat, "Your eye was bad and therefore you have been filled with darkness." We can build mega-businesses and create loads of wealth, but if our focus is chiefly upon this temporal age, these accomplishments will be filled with darkness.

An eternal focus releases light and revelation. When we focus on Jesus at the right hand of the Father, our body begins to be filled with light and revelation. Living with a good eye is waking up in the morning and focusing our attention upon pleasing the heart of God rather than pleasing ourselves. The good eye considers how to serve, give, and be a blessing to others at the expense of its own fleshly desires. When we live with a good eye, we will be filled with heavenly light, supernatural pleasure and delight. Oh, that we would be a people who are *filled with light*, that we would be fixed upon the eternal rather than upon those things that are temporal, carnal, and fading away!

The Spirit of Mammon

> No one can serve two masters; for either he will hate the one and love the other, or else he will be loyal to the one and despise the other. You cannot serve God and mammon. (Mt. 6:24)

Jesus admonishes His people to live lives that are simple, not given to extravagance and hoarding. It is unfortunate that many, even in the Church, spend their entire lives building a kingdom unto themselves. They consider how to become successful in this life and focus on their own comfort without considering the culture of the kingdom. They end up pursuing natural pleasures and owning lots of things that are luxurious, yet their lives are in complete opposition to Jesus' admonition in the Sermon on the Mount.

Jesus is addressing a mindset regarding the way that people think about their own personal pleasure. While He is addressing the way that people handle money, He is also focusing on the mentality that causes people to heap up treasures for themselves in this life. He is addressing the focus people have upon making their primary pursuit in this life attaining their own provision, pleasure, and comfort. When people live focused on pursuing their own pleasure, they are living according to the spirit of mammon. Mammon is not just money. Jesus uses mammon as a personification of the god of pleasure and riches. Mammon, therefore, is the desire for pleasure, riches, and all the things that make for your own comfort in this life.

In the West, our culture is possessed with the spirit

of mammon. In fact, the spirit of mammon is the spirit of the age. You can identify this influence easily through observing how people act with regard to their money and possessions. Have you ever walked into a bank and noticed that the people there seemed fairly uptight? Why are they acting this way? They are hypersensitive about their money. The reason they are so sensitive is because they do not want anyone to mess with their money! If you are messing with their money, you are messing with their livelihood. The unfortunate state of affairs is that their money is their lord. Jesus tells us not to make money, riches, or the desire for pleasures our focus in this life. Those who live their life striving for these things are serving the spirit of mammon. It is sad, but money, comfort, and pleasure have become their master.

Jesus wants us to understand we cannot serve God and mammon. The one who pursues the desire for pleasure is not serving God; he is serving mammon. Because we live in a Western culture so established upon the pursuit of riches, we tend to make allowances for ourselves regarding this clear biblical teaching. Many focus the entirety of their teaching ministry on "God's desire to make people wealthy," yet they rarely include the biblical warnings and admonitions to those who possess wealth. When we instruct people to "give in order to get" and to "use their faith" to receive bigger houses and nicer cars, are we following the value system of the kingdom of God? Are these pursuits congruent with biblical Christianity as explained by Jesus in the Sermon on the Mount?

The spirit of mammon is what causes people to live with a bad eye. The bad eye is focused on pleasing self and laying up treasures on the earth. The bad eye causes people to live for their own benefit and their immediate pleasure. When a person lives this way, they are under the sway of the spirit of mammon. The spirit of mammon encourages people to get the most pleasure out of life right now. The spirit of mammon drives people to get the biggest platform, the most notoriety, and the best job in order to acquire great riches in this life. This mentality is extremely similar to something we are all familiar with, the "American dream."

Think about the formula to accomplish the American dream: Get an education so you can get a good job, so you can get a lot of money, so you can retire at a young age, so you can live the rest of your life in pleasure. If you make enough money, then you can start your children off in exactly the same direction. We have reproduced this mentality generation after generation in America until we have made personal comfort and pleasure the greatest pursuit of life. The Declaration of Independence declares that we have an inalienable right to the "pursuit of happiness." However, the greatest pleasure anyone will ever experience in this life is the pursuit of the kingdom. Jesus' admonition in Matthew 6:33 is to pursue the kingdom and everything that you need will be freely given to you.

Our culture is primarily focused on pleasing self at the highest level possible. The pursuit of pleasures is the core value in serving the spirit of mammon. We must be delivered from the culture of this world system and renewed in our minds to the culture of the kingdom of God. We *cannot* serve God and mammon.

True Generosity

Freely you have received, freely give. (Mt. 10:8)

In order to come out from the sway of the spirit of mammon, we need to redefine our concept of generosity.

Many would agree that if we live off of eighty-five percent of our income and give away fifteen percent, we are being generous. This is especially true if we compare ourselves with how most people in the world live. However, there is a problem in how we define generosity. We tend to focus first on supplying all of our own needs, wants, and desires, and then we look to see how much money we have left over so that we may give some away. When this is our paradigm, we have once again been influenced by the spirit of mammon. Remember, mammon tells us to pursue our own provision, pleasure, and comfort above all else. So if we determine how much we are able to give based upon how much we have left after we have provided for all of our own desires, we are then operating according to the spirit of mammon.

Many people believe they cannot be generous because they do not have a lot of money. Many believe if they make a six-figure income, then they can afford to be generous. The truth is that generosity is not predicated upon the amount of money you possess. True generosity gives without regard to possessions. True generosity gives with a heart of gladness by the leading of the Spirit of the Lord. The foundational revelation of true generosity is understanding that all that we have received in this life has been given to us by God. When we realize all that we have has been given to us by heaven, then we will see ourselves as stewards of another Man's treasures. When this is our mentality, we will no longer strive in this life to acquire as much as possible for ourselves. When we see ourselves as provided for by God and stewards of His provision, then we will freely give without regard to what we have and without apprehension, because we will be confident that God is the One who provides all that we need (Mt. 6:31–33).

What does generosity look like to you? How do you know if someone is truly generous? Imagine that you and I are hiking together on a long journey that will take five days to complete. I have a supply of food that equals ten meals, and you have none. All ten meals have been given freely to me. If I gave you one meal and I kept nine and ate them over the course of our journey, would you consider me to be generous? What if I gave you two and consumed the other eight? Would you think of me as generous? Imagine it: I chow down eight meals while you barely get by on two. How much would I have to give away to be considered generous? What would generosity look like? What if I gave you five? Would that seem generous? What if I gave you six meals and only kept four for myself? We need to redefine generosity. We need to truly believe our Father loves us and provides for all of our needs. When we believe God is our Provider, generosity will become easy. We will be able to follow Jesus' words, "Freely you have received, now freely give."

Conclusion

What was working in the hearts of the believers in the early church that they would sell all they owned and put it at the apostles' feet? They wanted everything to be divided among the brethren so that no one would live without their needs being met. What if our leaders admonished us to live in the same manner? We would think they were cult leaders. This concept sounds so foreign to our ears because we are more in tune with the spirit of mammon than we are with the culture of the kingdom.

The disciples in the early church were combating the spirit of the age by living out the values of the kingdom of

God. Nothing could have seemed more foreign to them than to sell lands and homes that had been in their families for generations, yet they lived as people who were embracing true generosity and lifestyles of simplicity. They were in no way laying up for themselves treasures on the earth. They were, however, heaping up for themselves treasures in the kingdom. They were not all wealthy. You do not have to have a lot of money in order to be generous. They gave what they had. Remember the widow with the two mites (Mk. 12:42–44)? Jesus declared that she was the most generous of all.

We have tried to come up with a definition of generosity that allows us to mix the desire for our own personal pleasure and the pursuit of riches with giving very little of our excess to others. Real generosity cannot be combined with a focus on hoarding for one's self. Jesus said, "If you try to serve both God and mammon, you will hate one and serve the other." The word "other" literally means "the opposite." In other words, if you try to serve God and mammon, you will hate God and serve the opposite of God, mammon. God is as opposite to mammon as heaven is opposite to hell.

We must ask God to give us a vision of true generosity that is free from the sway of the spirit of mammon. It does not matter if you earn $600,000 or $6,000 a year. The issue is giving generously from a free heart that is not bound by the pursuit of personal preferences and carnal pleasures. Paul told Timothy, "Godliness with contentment is great gain" (1 Tim. 6:6). We must get a kingdom perspective on what true contentment is so that we may give generously of all we receive in this life. Jesus desires for us to be completely free from the spirit of mammon so that we may experience the greater riches of His kingdom.

CHAPTER 11
Judge Not

Judge not, that you be not judged. For with what judgment you judge, you will be judged; and with the measure you use, it will be measured back to you. And why do you look at the speck in your brother's eye, but do not consider the plank in your own eye? Or how can you say to your brother, 'Let me remove the speck from your eye'; and look, a plank is in your own eye? Hypocrite! First remove the plank from your own eye, and then you will see clearly to remove the speck from your brother's eye. (Mt. 7:1–5).

These verses have been quoted often and regularly misused. Many times, when a challenge has been issued to live righteously, people will respond with, "Judge not lest you be judged." This was not how Jesus intended these scriptures to be used. When they are used in this way, these verses become a crutch to embolden people to sin. Even though an individual may or may not truly believe that no one is allowed to call him to account for sin, he will use these verses to ease his own conscience when he is brought under conviction. Jesus never intended for His words to be used as a means to allow men to live without accountability. Nor did He mean that there are no circumstances in which people should judge others. In fact, in John 7:24, He encouraged His people to employ righteous judgment.

Righteous Judgment

> Do not judge according to appearance, but judge with righteous judgment. (Jn. 7:24).

If Jesus was not placing a universal prohibition on judging others, what then was He conveying through these words? He was calling His followers to righteousness and love, even through the difficult circumstance of bringing correction and judgment to another. He was setting a different course than the course the Pharisees had set for the people.

The religious leaders of that day were experts at placing "heavy burdens" and strict religious rules upon the people without actually practicing the rules themselves. As we discussed in an earlier chapter, they prescribed for the people a false system of righteousness based on man-made rules, yet they themselves did not even live what they prescribed. They continuously judged the people with severity and criticism in regard to sin, while they did not place themselves under the same scrutiny. By declaring, "Judge not that you be not judged," Jesus was taking aim at this mentality of severe religious judgment. He was issuing a warning to the religious leaders and laying out a guideline for believers to follow in regard to criticism and judgment.

A familiar feature of the sin nature is to exalt self and diminish others. When men become arrogant in their own righteousness, it is common for them to take the position of judge as it relates to the spirituality of another. Proverbs 20:6 declares that many men will speak of their own goodness. Jesus' admonition is to be careful how you judge because the manner in which you judge another will be applied to you by others. In other words, if you are harsh and critical in your judgment of other people, others will be harsh and critical of you when your motives or actions come into question. Jesus is conveying that when it comes time to judge, we should employ mercy and love. It is not that we should never call anyone to account for his actions. Nothing could be further from the truth. However, when we do bring accountability to another, we are to do it with a spirit of humility, love, and mercy. We are to speak truth in love and with grace.

If we enter into judgment without love as the centerpiece of our motives, we will fully miss the point of Jesus' admonitions about judging others. Love will always control and constrain us to seek the good of the other person, even when we have to bring accountability and judgment to them for their actions. If we are eager to rush to judgment against an individual, we are not operating in the culture of the kingdom of God. It is extremely possible for individuals to begin to embrace the Sermon on the Mount lifestyle and live out the values of the kingdom and then move right into self-righteousness and spiritual elitism. Jesus' warning to us is this: Do not judge others, thinking yourself to be better than they are. Examine yourself and check your own heart before you ever begin to judge someone else.

The Speck and the Plank

Examine yourselves as to whether you are in the faith. Test yourselves, that Jesus Christ is in you?— unless indeed you are disqualified. (2 Cor. 13:5)

The discussion regarding the speck and the plank is primarily about self-examination. The speck represents minor sin issues, while the plank represents major sin issues. He is trying to rid us of rushing to judgment against each other before we have thoroughly examined ourselves before the Lord.

When we rush to judgment with a critical spirit, we are guilty before God. The critical spirit looks at others and decides that every speck of sin that they have is a plank. A person with a critical spirit does not consider his own heart before God before he rushes to judgment. Those with a critical spirit have a great desire to identify the wrong in someone else without investigating their own hearts in such matters. They love to expose others because it strengthens them in their own self-righteousness. They will accuse another person in order to expose that one's sin without honestly considering their own state before God. Those with a critical spirit love to investigate and expose others but despise being investigated and exposed themselves. The one with a critical spirit hides behind a façade of religious piety, all the while harboring in his own life the same sins of which he accuses others. Those with a critical spirit are experts at identifying others' "specks" without ever considering that, before the Lord, their critical and judgmental attitude is a "plank" in their own eye. Who actually asks the Lord to investigate his own heart before he goes to another person to bring correction?

Jesus wants us to be rid of spiritual elitism and religious pride. Those who desire to live a Sermon on the Mount lifestyle must not begin to judge others who look like they are not yet fully embracing the value system of the kingdom. We must always look to ourselves before we ever make any assessment of someone else's spirituality. The questions remain: Should we ever make a judgment of another? Are there times when it is appropriate to judge? How do we call someone else to live the values of the kingdom without getting into elitism and a critical spirit?

The first thing we must realize is that from God's vantage point as it relates to us, our own sin is always a plank and someone else's sin is always a speck. His worldview is focused specifically on our lives and our individual choices for righteousness. God is chiefly concerned with conquering our hearts. Between God and us, He is firstly concerned with how we live. He always wants us to deal ruthlessly with the sin in our own lives and mercifully with the sin in another. You might say, "Now wait a minute. That guy is in adultery, and I just have a little lust issue." God says, "As it relates to you, the lust issue of your own heart is a plank, and the other man's issue is a speck. Let's deal with the lust in your own heart before you go rushing to judgment against someone else." When we realize that our own sin is a plank and the sin of others is a speck, it will keep us out of a critical spirit and enable us to deal mercifully with others who are in sin. It will aid us in ministering correction and judgment with love and humility rather than with criticism and condemnation. When we examine our own hearts before the Lord first, then He can use us to help remove the specks from our brothers' eyes.

We must consider the measure of mercy we use with others. It is essential we employ a generous measure of mercy when there is a need to bring correction or judgment, for the manner that we use to judge others will be the manner that is used to judge us. There is a great difference between operating in accusation with a critical spirit and mercifully appealing to another to change. We must realize that when we are bringing correction to another in the Church, we are dealing with another Man's wife. The Bride of Christ is just that—she is Jesus' wife. Though she may stray from the path of righteousness, He is still ravished over her. He is still faithfully committed to her. When we call her to righteous living, we should not use a long, pointy finger of accusation. We should earnestly implore her with a broken heart of weeping and lamentation. We should treat her with mercy and love while calling her to accountability in righteousness. God's prophetic messengers at the end of the age, who are commissioned to call the Bride to purity, will do so with brokenness and not brashness. They will operate in tenderness, not arrogance. They will treat the Church with the same concern and care that Jesus has for her. How severe will it be on the Day of judgment for the one who has mistreated Jesus' Bride?

Conclusion

When we have as much zeal to inspect ourselves as we have to correct others, then we will be used by God to help remove the specks in others. God wants us to act as a family of affection, understanding that we share the same condition. He wants us to see ourselves as part of the whole Body. Though the Body of Christ may be in great need and though it may be obvious that the Church has strayed from the path of righteousness, God wants us individually to take responsibility for our corporate condition. He wants us to be broken over the state of *our* sin. If we are graced with the privilege of calling His Bride to account, He wants us to do it with humility, not haughtiness—with kindness, not cruelty. When we speak the truth in love to one another, then, and only then, will we grow up together in Christ. Warring against one another with criticism and judgment is contrary to the culture of His kingdom. God desires us to realize that we are part of one another. He wants us to exhort one another to righteousness in a spirit of humility and meekness, rather than criticize each other from a heart full of judgment.

CHAPTER 12
A Collision Is Coming

Behold, I am coming as a thief. Blessed is he who watches, and keeps his garments, lest he walk naked and they see his shame. (Rev. 16:15)

I want to challenge you to a slow, meditative reading of the Sermon on the Mount with fasting and prayer. I know it will raise questions in your mind: Is this really the model for Christianity that Jesus wants us to live? How can we live this way when it seems so contrary to Western culture? Who is actually living out these values as the norm for their lives? We have so few models of this lifestyle in the West. Who will give himself unapologetically to Jesus' values and live contrary to the spirit of the age?

Contrast or Conformity

You are the salt of the earth; but if the salt loses its flavor, how shall it be seasoned? It is then good for nothing but to be thrown out and trampled underfoot by men. (Mt. 5:13)

After He lays out the core values, Jesus then calls those who are followers of His value system "the salt of the earth." Salt is a purifying and preserving agent. It is used to cleanse and to keep things from rotting. Jesus was calling those of His kingdom to embrace His value system and then live it out in the world. He was looking to create contrast between those who live His value system and those who embrace the spirit of the age. Today, He wants those of His kingdom to be so different from those of this world system that the distinction between the two is obvious. His subjects should have a purifying effect upon the culture of this world system. When the citizens of His kingdom live His values among those in the world, they will be salt.

There is a problem that arises when there is no contrast between those of His kingdom and those of the world system. He says, "When the salt loses its flavor, it is worthless." We must ask ourselves if the value system that we live is in obvious contrast to the spirit of the age raging all around us. Do we provide a purifying element to the culture? In other words, is the culture being changed because we are living the values of the kingdom? Or is the general value system in the Western church only slightly different from the world? Does there really appear to be a contradiction between the value system of the Church and that of the world? Are we truly salt? If we are so similar to the world that there is no distinct difference between us, I propose we have not truly embraced the values of the kingdom. Instead, we have embraced the spirit of the age. Oh, that we would not lose our purifying power because of conformity to a world system that is coming to an end.

The Western Crisis

> I beseech you therefore, brethren, by the mercies of God, that you present your bodies a living sacrifice, holy, acceptable to God, which is your reasonable service. And do not be conformed to this world, but be transformed by the renew-

ing of your mind, that you may prove what is that good and acceptable and perfect will of God. (Rom. 12:1–2)

Much of what we have produced through the church in the West does not carry the value system of the kingdom. We have Christian celebrities and TV personalities. We have TV shows and radio shows, seminars and seminaries, conferences and camps. We have built a billion-dollar, mega-ministry machine that continues to pump out books, CDs, teachings, music, videos, Bible schools, and churches everywhere. Yet we still have very few people living according to the value system of the kingdom of God. Where is the Church that is living the life of meekness and mourning, serving and giving, fasting and praying? We have taken the name of Jesus and painted it across our ministries, yet we have not lived the values that Jesus prescribed for those who would be citizens of His kingdom. If we are not living His value system, it begs the question: what value system have we embraced? Could it be that the church in the West has embraced the spirit of the age, mixed in some Christian language, and called it "Christ?" Has she rejected the very One who she claims to serve? We must take a serious look at the value system that we embrace, for if it does not look like the Sermon on the Mount, it is not the value system of the kingdom of God. We desperately need to return to the foundations of Christianity.

Some would say that I am being too "black and white" in my assessment and that we need to adapt to the culture in which we live in order to penetrate it with the gospel. I believe that we must come out from under the sway of the spirit of the age and be separated unto God in our values and lifestyles if we are going to have any authority to truly shift our culture. With a broken heart and through weeping in travail, I am calling us in the grace of God to return wholeheartedly to the Lord.

We must embrace the values of the kingdom without mixing in any of this world system. When we read the Sermon on the Mount, it becomes evident that most of our models of Christianity do not look anything like what Jesus prescribed. Often, because the disparity between how we live and what Jesus prescribed is so great, we reinterpret the Sermon on the Mount in a more palatable way in order to ease our consciences. We try to convince ourselves that Jesus did not really intend for us to be poor in spirit, meek, and mournful our whole lives; He just meant that we should acknowledge our general need for God. This is clearly not the case. Jesus, in no uncertain terms, taught us the standard values of His kingdom. If we do not embrace the values of His kingdom, the truth is that we do not embrace Him. As I've said before, the Sermon on the Mount expresses the very nature of Christ. When we embrace the culture of the kingdom, we become intimate with Jesus; we embrace Him. If we divorce ourselves from the values of the kingdom of God, we are not merely separating ourselves from a list of moral standards, we are divorcing ourselves from Christ.

When we try to interpret the Sermon on the Mount according to the spirit of the age, we lower the bar of the value system of the kingdom of God. In so doing, we no longer subscribe to the value system of Christ, but to the values of the spirit of this age, the culture of this world system. We must return with hearts that are rent, with fasting and weeping and mourning, and ask the Lord to deliver us from the spirit of the age and conform us to the image of His Son (Joel 2:12–13; Rom. 12:1–2). The level of our conformity to this world system is identified by the extent to which we live lives dissimilar to the values of the kingdom of God. We cannot continue to allow the Sermon on the Mount to be clichéd or trite in our minds. The values of the Sermon on the Mount must become central to everything we do.

Two Paths

> Enter by the narrow gate; for wide is the gate and broad is the way that leads to destruction, and there are many who go in by it. Because narrow is the gate and difficult is the way which leads to life, and there are few who find it. (Mt. 7:13–14)

There are two paths that are before us in the Church. These two courses seem so similar because they appear to bring us to similar ends. One path is the spirit of the age, and the other is the value system of Christ. Each is focused on bringing greatness to humanity. One is focused on the greatness we can attain in this age, while the other is focused on human greatness in the age to come. The one who walks the narrow path will rule with Jesus upon His throne with the authority of the Father in the age to come. The other who embraces the spirit of this age is driven to make himself great in this life. Jesus says, "Push back from trying to be great in this life and make someone else great at the expense of yourself. Serve and bless others in meekness, and you will inherit the earth." The spirit of this age instructs us to do whatever it takes to get to the top, even if it means stepping on others in order to make ourselves great. One path requires you to put aside your own desires now for the benefit of others. The other path encourages you to do all you can now for your own benefit. At a glance, the two paths do look similar, but they are not. The spirit of the age is the broad path; the value system of Christ is the narrow way.

We must become aware of the sway of the spirit of the age within the Church. We have not been aware of how the spirit of the age has influenced us to try to make ourselves great in this age. Many use scriptures out of context to insist we should be heaped with blessings and riches in this life. While it is clear that God wants to bless His people, the Western mentality of blessing is in direct contradiction to the values of His kingdom. Jesus' value system calls us to humble ourselves in this life so that He can exalt us in the age to come (Jas. 4:10; 1 Pet. 5:6).

The Coming Collision

> Behold, I am coming quickly! Hold fast what you have, that no one may take your crown. (Rev. 3:11)

Who leads like Jesus? If you and I were starting a new business, it is extremely unlikely that we would choose spiritual poverty, spiritual mourning, meekness, hunger for righteousness, mercy, purity in heart, peacemaking, and persecution as the core values of our company. However, this is the value system Jesus employs in order to set up His global empire. If you and I were going to build a company, we would look for the strongest, boldest leaders who would create the biggest stir and make the most financial impact. Jesus looks for the one who is poor in spirit and meek (Isa. 66:2). Jesus doesn't think the way we think, and He will not build His empire on human strength. He is building His global empire with living stones, yet only ones that have been broken.

Jesus is not the kind of king who says, "This is what's important to me, but if you don't think it's important, that's okay. We'll do what you want to do instead." Jesus embraced torture and death on the cross so that we would be able to embrace what He values. When I see His value system from the Sermon on the Mount and then consider Western Christianity, it becomes obvious that the two are in absolute conflict. We must decide whether or not the Bible is the Word of God. If it is, then we must become aggressive about living the lifestyle Jesus set forth in the Sermon on the Mount. When we label ourselves as Christ's and yet do not embrace His culture and value system, we are setting ourselves up for a collision. Those who embrace the spirit of this age and call themselves by the name of Christ will collide directly with the Man Christ Jesus.

Beloved, there is an inevitable collision coming! It is directly ahead of us. These two cultures will not continue to co-exist under the banner of Christ. Where people use the name of Christ and do not embrace His values, a crash is inevitable. There will be great turmoil within the Church between those who want the values of the kingdom and those who want a Western version of Christianity. The values of Christ's heart will become the central issue. Men will divide over whether or not His values should be embraced as the foundation for normal Christianity.

There is a collision coming! The Lord is going to press the Church, allowing her incongruence and inconsistencies to be exposed. Trials, challenges, judgment events, and persecutions will arise. Persecution from the religious community and challenges from the world are going to heat the furnace in order to purify the Bride at the end of the age.

Jesus is coming to take leadership of His kingdom! In that hour His Bride will not be possessed with the spirit of the age. He will see to it that every bit of mixture is removed from her. He is going to purify her and have for Himself a spotless Church without blemish. She will not embrace another value system in that day. She will only subscribe to the values of her King. He will stop at nothing to remove from her all that is not of His nature. Beloved, we must get ready, for a collision is coming!

Conclusion

Oh, how we need deliverance! We need to be delivered from the course of this world system. We need to be delivered from the spirit of the age. The spirit of this age always allures us to immediate gratification. It attempts to circumvent us in the process of maturity in Christ. It says, "Do you want to be great? Do you want to have riches, fame, power, and pleasure? Here is the answer: pursue it now by fulfilling the desires of your flesh." This path is contradictory to God's design. God has designed for us to be great through partnering with His Son. Just as Jesus became humble to the point of death and then God highly exalted Him, so it is the same for all those who are citizens of His kingdom.

It has become commonplace for us to take the principles that have caused businesses to succeed and bring them right into the Church. We often attend "success seminars" in order to find out how to expand our ministries. I believe such seminars simply teach us how to maneuver and manipulate men through the sway of the spirit of this age. Through ministry personas that we have enthroned, we have taught our young ones to pray in order to get anointed so that they can have a big ministry platform. Somehow the definition for success in the Church has become the size of your ministry platform and budget. I have met many young ministers who simply want to "make it big" so that they can get on the ministry circuit and become a sought after ministry personality. I tell you, this mentality is the spirit of the age, and we must be delivered from it.

The Lord is going to sweep across the Church in order to remove our conformity to this world system. He is going to give us the option to embrace His value system or continue along under the sway of the spirit of the age. If we do not embrace the value system of the kingdom, we will collide with Jesus. He is going to shake everything that can be shaken until everyone comes under the authority of the kingdom of God (Hag. 2:21–22). There is a collision coming! He is going to remove everything that is not according to His culture. I pray that you would ask God to give you the grace to identify the areas of compromise in your own life so that you may depart from the sway of the spirit of the age and truly embrace the values of the kingdom of God.

IHOP Atlanta
MISSIONS BASE

On February 12, 2006, a prayer and worship meeting began in Atlanta that continues to this very hour. Since that day, night and day worship and intercession have continually ascended to the throne of God from Atlanta. Convinced that Jesus is worthy of ceaseless worship, men and women of all ages are giving themselves to lives of extravagant devotion expressed through 24/7 prayer. Structured in eighty-four, two-hour prayer meetings per week, full teams of musicians, singers, and intercessors lift their voices in praise and supplication, asking God to fulfill His promise and give the nations of the earth to Jesus as His inheritance.

IHOP–Atlanta is a ministry serving the entire metro-Atlanta area, open twenty-four hours a day for any person or group desiring to come at any time to worship and pray individually or corporately. The prayer room is the heartbeat of all that goes on at the IHOP–Atlanta Missions Base. Each prayer meeting follows one of four formats: devotional worship, prophetic worship, worship with the Word, or intercession.

Visiting IHOP–Atlanta

One-day Seminars: These intense one-day trainings are held on the first Saturday of each month. Topics of study include "Growing in the Spirit of Prophecy," "Omega—Studies in the End Times," "Passion for Jesus," and "The Harp and Bowl Model of Worship and Intercession." Registration is available online at www.ihop-atlanta.com.

Encounter Services: Services are held every Sunday at 10:00 am and 6:00 pm. The IHOP–Atlanta Encounter Service is a unique gathering that provides an atmosphere of freedom of worship, instruction, and exhortation from the Word, as well as prophetic impartation. Each service incorporates prophetic worship, biblical teaching, prayer, and ministry times. These weekly times of encounter are heavily dependent on the grace and leading of the Holy Spirit. Each service is geared to calling individuals to a depth of the knowledge of God, intimacy with Jesus, urgency for the hour, and the Sermon on the Mount lifestyle.

Internships

The goal of the International House of Prayer–Atlanta internships is to equip individuals in the messages of intimacy with Jesus, urgency for the hour, and the Sermon on the Mount lifestyle. Each internship affords the individual the opportunity to live in the environment of night and day prayer as an intercessory missionary with structured times of fasting and prayer, outreach, instruction, and impartation.

Intro: A three-month, daytime training program for all ages, married or single.

The Watch Internship: A three-month internship for ages 18-30 taking place during the NightWatch, from midnight to 6:00 am.

The Pursuit Internship: A three-month daytime internship for young adults ages 18-25.

The Nitro Internship: A three-month internship for married couples and singles taking place during the NightWatch, from midnight to 6:00 am.

The Joshua Internship: A three-month daytime internship for adults 50 and older.

Encounter Teen Camp: A one-week program held each summer to equip teens in prophetic worship, intercession, and intimacy with Jesus.

Gatekeeper School of Ministry

Gatekeeper School of Ministry is a part-time ministry school focused on equipping forerunners with urgency for the hour and intimacy with God. Intimacy and urgency release profound conviction for the necessity of night and day worship and prayer. Students are challenged to approach the Word of God with a collegiate academic zeal, while maintaining a devotional spirit bathed in the atmosphere of 24/7 worship and intercession. In this unique environment, revelation of the Word goes deep into the heart causing the student to grow in the knowledge of God. Three 12-week trimesters are offered annually.

Visit the IHOP–Atlanta website for more information

WWW.IHOP-ATLANTA.COM

Podcasts, MP3 Downloads, Prayer Room Blogs, Internship Applications, Seminar Registration, School of Ministry, Upcoming Events, Conferences, and More…

International House of Prayer
Missions Base of Kansas City

24/7 Live Worship and Prayer
IHOP.org

Since September 19, 1999, we have continued in night and day prayer with worship as the foundation of our ministry to win the lost, heal the sick, and make disciples, as we labor alongside the larger Body of Christ to see the Great Commission fulfilled and to function as forerunners who prepare the way for the return of Jesus. By the grace of God, we are committed to combining 24/7 prayers for justice with 24/7 works of justice until the Lord returns. We do this best as our lives are rooted in prayer that focuses on intimacy with God and intercession for breakthrough of the fullness of God's power and purpose for this generation.

For more information on our internships, conferences, university, live prayer room webcast, and more, please visit our website at IHOP.org.

International House of Prayer Missions Base
3535 E. Red Bridge Road, Kansas City, MO 64137
816.763.0200 • info@ihop.org • IHOP.org

IHOPU

International House of Prayer University

Ministry, Music, Media, and eSchool
IHOP.org/university

The International House of Prayer University (IHOPU) is a full-time Bible school which exists to equip this generation in the knowledge of God and the power of the Spirit for the bold proclamation of the Lord Jesus and His return.

Students embrace rigorous theological training and Sermon on the Mount lifestyles in the context of a thriving missions base fueled by night and day prayer (IHOP–KC). As a result, theological education obtained in the classroom is intrinsically connected to intimacy with Jesus and hands-on experience.

IHOPU is distinct from many other institutions of higher learning in the United States in that we seek a holistic approach to education with an emphasis on the forerunner ministry, and a NightWatch training element. IHOPU is led by intercessory missionaries in an environment of night and day prayer and a thriving missions base.

International House of Prayer University
3535 E. Red Bridge Road, Kansas City, MO 64137
816.763.0243 • ihopu@ihop.org • IHOP.org/university